Music, Anxiety & Me

How To Transform Your Life By Learning The Violin!

Hazel Spain

Disclaimer:

FREEDOM Book Publishing Limited

Author; Hazel Spain Title: Music, Anxiety & Me

PAPERBACK ISBN: 978-1-8381556-4-3
E-BOOK ISBN: 978-1-8381556-5-0

Category: Self help - Music

FREEDOM Book Publishing

Book Interior and Cover Designer: Hammad Khalid

LEARN THE VIOLIN!

To get the best experience with this book, I've found readers who download and use my **ULTIMATE BEGINNER'S COURSE FOR VIOLIN** are able to implement faster and take the next steps needed to fast-track their musical success!

You can access the course at:

www.hazelsviolinschool.com

Disclaimer

I have tried to recreate events, locales and conversations from my memories of them. In order to maintain their anonymity in some instances I have changed the names of individuals and places, I may have changed some identifying characteristics and details such as physical properties, occupations and places of residence.

Dedication

To my long suffering grandparents, Mamie and Willie Collins. In your sixties, after raising three 'spirited' boys, you unexpectedly became parents again and welcomed into your home a baby girl, whom you nurtured and cherished. Gran you were, and still are, my first and true best friend; my soul mate. I love you to the ends of the earth, and there isn't a day that goes by where I don't think about and miss you.

My dear Papa, thank you wholeheartedly stepping in and becoming my dad when I needed you most. Whilst I wish every day that you were still here, I feel incredibly grateful to have had you in my life for twenty-seven years. Thank you for being the funniest, silliest, most gentle and loving father I could have asked for.

Thank you both for being my biggest fans.

What People Are Saying About This Book

A beautifully written autobiography. Hazel is a natural writer, the candid and honest account of her life - raw, tragic, and sometimes even brutal, should be difficult to read but instead you'll find yourself inspired, engaged and rooting for her until the very end.

Her openness about anxiety is refreshing, and it feels like her story should take centre stage in a series about humans, the power of music and the enduring strength of a brave spirit.

(Gran and Papa would be proud. It is a testament to their amazing love and devotion that has made all the difference in the life of a child, a talented musician and now a gifted writer).

Jiki Lim Ford
Friend & Freelance Producer – BBC Scotland.

Your words are so captivating and I felt a really deep connection to you - as if I was present whilst you were living your life.

Sidra Khan

Hazel demonstrates the sheer power that playing an instrument can have, through a candid, heartfelt expo-

sition of a life guided by the violin strings. The reader is swept along by the poignant harmony of a talented musician and her music, the intensity of their bond both inspiring and intriguing, as she gracefully navigates the peaks and valleys of a remarkable life. The fundamental message Hazel delivers with a punch is this: playing music is for anyone and everyone, and it could change the course of a life.

Ellie Grace Solomon

From your unsettled beginnings to the young successful mother you've become today is a credit to your true grit and determination to succeed and devote your life to your true love, the Violin! Music has been your strength throughout your journey and your resilience in the face of adversity continues to shine.

Through your story we laughed and we cried and have learned so much more about the woman who came into our lives as a 3-month-old baby. With unreserved love Simon and Liz

Simon & Liz Farmer

Hazel's book affirms the value of learning a musical instrument for all sorts of reasons... including overcoming anxiety, having access to incredible experiences, opening the door to friendships, and not to forget the pure joy of creating music. Her honest and straight forward story telling gives the reader a real insight into her life; that of a violinist and lover of music to her core.

Fellow pupil and flautist from Hazel's years at The Music School of Douglas Academy

A fantastic, heartfelt account of Hazel's life and love for the violin. Hazel's honesty and sharing of her career is inspiring, this book is such an uplifting read for all music lovers. Having recently revisited the violin, I have been lucky enough to have Hazel as my teacher. Hazel's knowledge and eye for detail has made me a much more confident performer and has sparked my love for the violin all over again. Thank you for creating this wonderful read!

K. L. Cochrane

A brave and thought-provoking insight into the journey of a musician. This heartfelt and painfully personal tale highlights the power of music and proves how a clear progression through hard work can provide solace in the darkest of times. Any parent of a troubled child who shows an aptitude for music can read this first-hand account and know that there is light at the end of the tunnel.

Band Sergeant Sarah Paxton, (Flautist)

Foreword

My first recollection of Hazel was of an attractive, petite young girl walking into my consulting studio with a violin on her back, looking to all intents and purposes like a seasoned violinist. Little did I know that despite bringing her violin to every session, it would take many weeks before she felt able to take it out of its case.

Hazel's story is a refreshingly honest, but sadly rare, account of the struggles experienced by many musicians as they battle with stress and anxiety. It is an inspirational account of a young person whose love for her violin and music brought much needed self-worth and focus to her life. At the same time, her story shows how that love can be eroded if self-worth is based primarily on the quality of playing and performance.

This book is unique in that it brings together the two opposing sides of music, the therapeutic qualities of music which are well documented and the emotional and physical strain that is often experienced by the musicians who serve music. Unfortunately, the stigma attached to the latter means that physical and mental stress is rarely discussed, either by student or professional musicians, unless a crisis or burn-out occurs. A loss of love for music (or as Hazel describes it, being unable to feel music), is a common feature of anxiety whereby a much-loved instrument can become the centre of a love/hate relationship.

What has yet to be fully addressed in research and practise, and what Hazel's story highlights, is the need for a greater understanding of the complex relationship between the intrinsic love of music which motivates young people to take up an instrument and partake in musical activities and the impact that the pressures associated with serving the music has on that love.

Charities such as BAPAM and Helpmusicians provide expert and affordable help to any musician who needs it. Their seminars and on-line resources emphasise the need for all musicians to adopt a healthy approach to music making and encourage lifestyle choices which can help manage their physical and psychological wellbeing. Educational institutions are slowly incorporating a more holistic approach to musical training where greater attention is given to the health and wellbeing of students. Hopefully in time, these efforts may filter into the culture of the profession.

However, you do not need to become a professional musician to enjoy the love of an instrument. You do not need to perform music in public to express yourself through a musical instrument. We live in anxious times and worryingly, statistics from the Mental Health Foundation show a marked increase in diagnosed anxiety and depression particularly in age group 5-19. Of course, the reasons for this are varied and complex but recommended interventions do not include musical participation. It is extremely unfortunate and short-sighted that learning a musical instrument is of low priority in the state school system and that the resources music has to offer young people are not recognised in helping them cope with day to day pressures. I doubt this will change in the short term but initiatives such as Hazel's are a welcome step towards making music accessible to everyone, irrespective of their background or social status.

'Things get broken to get better', or in the context of Post Traumatic Growth Theory (Payne et al.2007) if a precious vase breaks you have three choices. You can dispose of it or you can glue it back together, but it will be fragile and never quite the same. Alternatively, you can create a beautiful mosaic from the pieces. I applaud Hazel for her courage in telling her story, but most of all I applaud her for her strength and determination in overcoming huge adversity in her young life. It is only by experiencing adversity that we can develop the resilience to engage with our anxieties, manage negative emotions and aspire to creating that beautiful mosaic which helps us grow into confident and capable human beings.

Dr Jane Oakland

Dorset

2020

References

Payne, A.J., Joseph, S. & Tudway, J. (2007) Assimilation and accommodation processes following traumatic experiences. Journal of Loss and Trauma. 12: 75-91

Contents

Introduction

I never imagined I would write a book. I took part in a book writing challenge for fun, and to give me something positive to focus my attention on whilst the UK was in lockdown during the Coronavirus Pandemic of 2020. I never actually imagined I'd finish the book, let alone have it published. Nevertheless, all I can say is that I'm glad I persevered, as it's turned out to be rather therapeutic to put pen to paper, and to sift through the past twenty-nine years of my life.

Come to think of it, I'm not sure if even my closest friends know much of my story. This is probably in part down to the fact that I haven't broadcasted it from the rooftops (I mean, let's face it, there are way more interesting people out there than me), but also because over the years I've gotten used to just repeating the same vague thing over and over again, omitting and smoothing over any unpleasant or awkward bits, and after a while, it just becomes the go-to script. Hopefully I'm not alone in doing this. I think it's what we all do to an extent?

Some of you may know that I am a professional violinist and hold a degree in music from the Royal Conservatoire of Scotland. I set up my business, 'Hazel's Violin School' in December 2019, with the aim of bringing the violin to a wider audience and to create resources for people who wouldn't normally be in a position to learn. This could be for any number of reasons. I'm strongly of the belief that anyone and EVERYONE should be given the opportunity to learn a musical instrument, which is why I tailor my lessons and courses to make them as accessible as possible and why I teach the violin in a variety of settings and in various ways.

Ways to Learn With Me

- With the **Free BONUS Course** linked the end of this book. If you can't wait any longer, flip to the end now!
- With the **Hazel's Violin School Online Membership** where you will enjoy **FREE ACCESS** to my Beginner Adults Violin Course and Beginner Children's Violin Course worth £97 PLUS discounted access to all future online courses and **LIFETIME ACCESS** to the exclusive **LEARN VIOLIN FAST!** Private members' Facebook Community where you can upload progress videos and gain feedback from myself and other members of the group. **In addition to this** there will be monthly masterclasses, tutorials, competitions and giveaways! To find out more visit: www.hazelsviolinschool.com
- Through **Hazel's VIPs** – my premium online **one-to-one mentoring** programme run over **90 days** where you will receive one-to-one weekly lessons from me - everything you will need from me as a violin teacher with lessons tailored to your specific goals! To find out more visit: www.hazelsviolinschool.com

I teach beginners all the way through to advanced students. I teach children from the age of four all the way through to those who are in their retirement. My FREE private members' group on Facebook 'Learn Violin FAST' has members from all over the world and is a lovely, positive community where members can gather to celebrate the joys of music and learning the violin. **If you would like to sign up to the Hazel's Violin School Online Membership** and be automatically added to the group, please follow this link www.hazels-violinschool.com

I can't wait to welcome you!

As the violin played such a huge part in my life growing up, and is predominantly responsible for how my life has turned out, I felt it important to spread the message that no matter which obstacles you may be facing in your life, and no matter how impossible your circumstances may seem, learning a musical instrument can open up many doors and opportunities you never thought possible. I want to show you that you don't have to come from a privileged background to go to music school and music college, and to tell you that no matter what life throws at you, if you have a passion for something and a skill, no one can ever take that away from you. So much good has come to me from learning the violin. Here are a few of the benefits:

How learning the violin has improved my life

- It has taught me lifelong self-discipline.
- It's how I've met some of my closest friends.
- It introduced me to my husband and now I have a beautiful son.
- It's enabled me to travel.
- It's made me resilient.
- I've been on television and been an extra in a film.

- It's enabled me to have the lifestyle I have today, and to own a business I'm passionate about.

As you have probably gathered, it hasn't all been easy. In fact, a lot of it has been really hard. I have suffered crippling anxiety since I was a child, and it's thanks to the violin that for the most part, I have recovered.

How learning the violin can improve your mental health

- Improved social life/gives you the opportunity to meet amazing, inspiring people.
- Strengthens memory and improves cognitive functioning.
- Reduced anxiety and depression (I can attest to this).
- Gives you tangible goals to work towards.
- It's fun = makes you happy = 'feel-good'.
- Provides a sense of achievement.
- Builds confidence.
- Practising improves patience.
- Increases creativity in other areas.

So, why am I writing this book?

I am writing this book, because I want to share with you my experience of how music and the violin helped me overcome some of the toughest years of my life, most of which were brought on by a degree of instability in my early childhood.

Although this book is predominantly directed towards parents who are looking for ways to help their children overcome stress, anxiety or low mood, I believe that this book can benefit anyone who struggles with their mental health. So, whether you are reading this as a parent or for yourself, no matter what stage you are at in your life and no matter what you may be facing right now, I hope that by the end you will feel encouraged to consider using a musical instrument as an aid in mental health recovery, and to discover for yourself how music can be used as a powerful tool in helping overcome mental health obstacles by providing a source of comfort, self-purpose and creativity which can always be accessed in harsh times.

(Yet another) Disclaimer

Let me be clear, this book is in no way intended as an alternative to conventional therapy methods, and seeking help from a mental health professional is absolutely crucial in promoting a quicker and smoother recovery. You will discover through reading my own story that a large portion of my recovery is thanks to my grandparents seeking professional help for me in the form of a child psychologist, and even later on in my life I have sought professional help on more than one occasion. So, whilst music and the violin can work tremendously in conjunction with traditional therapy methods, supporting and accelerating the recovery process, it shouldn't be relied upon as a method of therapy in its own right.

Before I go any further, I should mention that my dear grandparents sadly passed away in 2018. I won't go into it too much at this stage, as it's still quite raw, but they passed away within a few months of each other after both having suffered relatively short illnesses. It was truly awful, and completely unexpected. It took me a while to get my head around, and although each day is becoming easier, their passing has left me shell-shocked to say the least. Every day is another day toward acceptance, and I know that in time things will get easier, but at present, I'm still reeling from the experience. This is actually another reason why I'm throwing myself into my work and my violin practice. In immersing myself in the violin, I always find the solace I need.

In the twenty years that I have been playing the violin, I have been teaching for nearly thirteen of them. At the time of writing this book, I am almost thirty years old. Thanks to my wonderful violin teacher, Christine Alves - who initially introduced me to the violin when I was a nervous eight –year-old - and to Anna Markov, who nurtured my playing through secondary school and music college, I now feel so blessed to be able to say that throughout the years and throughout my experiences as a violinist, I have been taught and educated by some of the very best tutors from around the world.

FREE BONUS

At the end of the book, there will be a link that will direct you to the free violin course that accompanies this book. This is designed for those of you who have connected with my journey and would like to start learning the violin from home. Whether you are reading this and want to teach yourself, or whether you are a parent hoping to introduce your child to the basics, this easy-to-follow guide will cover everything you need to know - from where to source your very first violin, to setting up a solid technique and preparing to play your very first piece of music. Again, although this guide is predominantly geared towards parents, the videos are not childish, and the same information can be applied to adults who would like a brief introduction to the violin for themselves.

So, to summarise, there are many reasons why I'm writing this book. I wanted to connect with my pupils and with you, the reader. I wanted to document some of my past in the hope that I can help and inspire even just one person who might be feeling lost. I wanted to show how you could get started with the very basics of the violin from the comfort and familiarity of your own home, before having to think about spending a penny on a teacher. This will hopefully be of great help to individuals and to those of you with children who are shy, anxious or who struggle with new environments.

Ultimately, I want to prove to you that no matter which curveballs life throws in your path, if you have a passion for something and skill, no one can ever take that away. Playing a musical instrument has the ability to help a person escape their current reality, both mentally and physically. It can open up doors and opportunities you never thought imaginable. It can introduce you to some of the most influential and inspiring people you will ever meet. It really can change the course of your life.

Who this book is for:

- Parents whose children struggle with stress, anxiety, low mood or any other mental health issues.
- Parents whose children have come through or are experiencing trauma or stressful events i.e. grief, loss, divorce etc.

- Individuals who are looking for new ways to tackle mental health.
- Anyone who is going through a tough time, from everyday disappointments to varying mood disorders.
- Anyone who is interested in education, in particular music education and the benefits of learning a musical instrument.
- Any parent who wants to help better understand their child.
- Anyone who is interested in child psychology, education or child development.
- Teachers/Foster parents/adoptive parents/guardians/social workers/outreach workers/education providers.
- Grandparents who are becoming parents again.
- Violin teachers who want to better understand their students.
- And finally, anyone who wants to learn the violin! Yes, even if you aren't interested in the anxiety stuff, flip straight to the back to receive your first introduction to learning the violin!

Who this book is NOT for:

- Those looking for a substitute or alternative to conventional therapies or treatments.
- Those looking for advanced violin tuition (there will be another book for this!)

Prologue

I'll never forget my first experience of teaching a pupil. I was seventeen, and it was slap bang in the middle of the that luxurious period of time where I had just finished high school and was waiting to start music college in the autumn. It was completely by chance, and to my mind, I was nowhere near ready to teach anyone.

He was a boy of around nine or ten, and he was preparing to audition for a specialist music school in Aberdeen. I'll call him Finn. I can't remember the ins and outs of why my teacher, Anna had been called away so unexpectedly, but I do remember there being a situation whereby this important audition was looming for Finn, and Anna was having to miss a few lessons in the lead-up to it. It was unlike Anna to miss anything important her students did, so I knew it was a big deal that she was asking me to take over her teaching for a couple of weeks. I remember nervously waiting in my grandparents' living room for Finn and his dad to arrive, wondering what on earth I was going to do or say to either of them.

Finally, a car pulled up alongside the house, and I knew they had arrived. It was so strange to see anyone or anything different on our street back home. Although my grandparents' house looked out directly onto the busy Dumbarton Road, it was unusual for anything out of the ordinary to happen there. That day, when the unfamiliar car drew up outside and a little boy emerged with a violin case, I quickly rushed to answer the door. No doubt, the curtain-twitchers were out in full force that day, hoping to catch a glimpse something interesting. By the way, 'Curtain-twitchers' is a name I made up for nosy neighbours. Our street back home was full of them, and I suddenly felt protective towards my new guests.

As I ushered them both into my grandparents' living room, I couldn't help but notice that Finn and his dad seemed to be total opposites of each another. Whilst Finn's dad was jovial and unfazed, Finn was more reserved and stood in silence as he looked up at me with solemn brown eyes. Instantly, it occurred to me that the boy was probably rather daunted in these unfamiliar surroundings. I'm not sure what came over me, as I too was often shy around new people, but somehow intuition kicked in and told me I needed to put the little boy at ease. From that moment onwards, I was in 'teacher mode'. I encouraged Finn to take his violin out, and I went through to the kitchen make his dad a cup of tea as he did so. We tuned up; we chatted some more. I could see Finn was beginning to relax.

Probably within the first ten minutes or so, I realised I could do this job for the rest of my life. There I was, sitting in my grandparents' living room, listening to a talented little boy tackle tricky audition pieces. I was in my element. I must have only taught Finn for a few weeks, but I remember feeling a surge of pride when I was told that he had been accepted into the music school.

I realise now how incredibly lucky I was to have been taught by one of the most respected violin teachers in the UK, and how privileged I was to be asked to teach one of her pupils. It goes without saying that Finn's success back then could only be attributed to Anna and obviously Finn himself, but the sense of achievement it gave me knowing that I had played a small part in the boy's success was inspirational and a pivotal moment in my life.

Time passed, and I continued to teach throughout my music college years. I always loved teaching my students and the mixture of ages and abilities. I loved how teaching such a varied group of people imparted onto me how to become versatile as a teacher, and how in teaching others, I was constantly learning myself. One minute I'd be teaching a young child, or a high school pupil, and the next I'd be working with someone in their thirties looking for a way to de-stress from their hectic lives, or someone who had retired and taken up a new hobby. I think the oldest pupil I had was over seventy, and the youngest has been around four.

Following Finn's lessons, Anna urged me to find some of my own pupils to teach, and remarked that with experience, I could become a rather sought-after violin teacher. As time passed, Anna would look for opportunities for me within teaching and often impart her own wisdom upon me during our lessons together. I was eager to teach and keen to learn more, although once music college started, my priorities quickly began to change as my head became saturated with essay deadlines and performance exams. So, whilst I continued to teach throughout my time at music college, it wouldn't be until years later that I'd be making it my sole focus.

In 2017, nearly ten years after my first lessons with Finn and five years following my graduation from the Royal Conservatoire of Scotland, I found myself back at the Conservatoire's concert hall – there to take part in a memorial concert celebrating the life and works of a well-known and highly esteemed Scottish violin maker. It was a beautiful event, arranged and hosted by Anna to showcase the violin maker's life's work. The man's family, along with musicians from all over Scotland had been invited to come and pay homage to the exceptionally talented luthier who had tragically passed away earlier that year, leaving behind a young family along with many heartbroken colleagues and friends. The idea behind the concert was that it would feature all of his beautiful instruments, allowing them to be seen and heard in all their glory. People came to celebrate, marvel and appreciate this man's instruments, and the concert itself featured many talented artists, both soloists and ensemble groups. I was invited to play in the main, larger ensemble, which consisted of players from all over the country who had been lucky enough to own an instrument made by this exceptionally talented man. It was awe-inspiring, as people of all ages and stages in their career had gathered to celebrate this wonderful figure.

As I entered the hall, I saw many familiar faces, including Anna who waved excitedly, and my old friend Katy Sullivan, whom I'd graduated with back in 2012. Katy and I made our way over to the stage, chatting animatedly, eager to catch up having not seen each other since graduation, as not so soon after that we had both gotten married and gone our separate ways.

The music stands were all laid out with our names and the music we would be playing sitting upon them.

The hall was buzzing with excitement, and despite it being tinged with a real sadness, everyone was just so pleased to be there and to be celebrating such a well-respected figure in the music industry. As Katy and I approached the music stands, we realised that we weren't going to be 'desk buddies' so gave each other a little wave and arranged to meet for lunch after the rehearsal. As I lifted my violin up onto my shoulder and began to tune up, I spotted a tall, dark-haired boy of around seventeen, walking towards me with a violin under his arm. This must be my desk partner, I thought, musing that although I had never met him, he looked vaguely familiar. 'Hi, I'm Hazel', I said, looking up at the young boy who was towering above me. He smiled and his dark brown eyes shone. 'I know', he responded. 'I'm Finn, you taught me when I was little.'

What Is Anxiety?

Did you know that anxiety is considered to be one of the most common mental health problems in the UK? In England, one in four people will experience a mental health problem of some kind, with one in six stating that they have experienced a common mental health problem such as anxiety or depression in any given week.

If I were to try and explain anxiety to a non-sufferer, it would go something like this. Anxiety is just another word for feeling scared or worried. Most of us will feel this way at some point in our lives, especially if we are being faced with a stressful situation. Our brains are really clever in that they have an in-built alarm bell function, which is really useful for telling us when something in our world isn't right and needs to be addressed. In other words, our brain basically wants this situation to go away as quickly as possible, so it sends out signals to our body which kick-starts our body's automatic danger response system, otherwise known as the 'Fight, Flight or Freeze' response, or 'FFF' for short. I know, pretty cool, right? But when it's actually happening to you, it's no walk in the park, I promise! Whilst this experience can be deeply uncomfortable, and, for most people downright terrifying, this sequence of dramatic physical changes that happen within our bodies are actually designed to help and protect us by increasing our awareness and prompting us to deal with emergencies, like that time we had to swerve our car to avoid the nutcase coming towards us on the wrong side of the road. I hope to goodness this has never actually happened to you, but hopefully you catch my drift! Just as quickly as it came, once the acute stress is over, our bodies quickly revert back to normal.

I often imagine anxiety as sitting on a spectrum. Regular anxiety that is experienced by most people, and generally isn't considered to be an anxiety disorder, and would sit at the lower end of the spectrum. This type of anxiety is usually experienced as low levels of worry, uncertainty or apprehension, and is often accompanied by mild physical symptoms like muscle tension, shallow breathing and increased heart rate. Psychologically, it can present itself as something like doubting your ability to go somewhere or complete a task. The main thing to remember here is that once the stressful event is over; the milder symptoms of anxiety generally pass without consequence, and don't tend to negatively affect a person's day-to-day ability to function. Actually, these mild symptoms of anxiety might even have a positive effect on our levels of concentration and capacity to problem-solve, whilst inspiring us to work harder towards personal goals. Also, let's not forget that occasionally mild anxiety might do its job and actually aid in making us aware of potential hazards in our environment, such as perhaps we might just decide to take the elevator that day as opposed to the rickety-looking staircase which looks unsafe.

On the other hand, higher levels of anxiety tend to fall towards the other end of the spectrum, and anxiety that has been diagnosed occurs when a person's anxiety levels rise enough to impact and interfere with their everyday lives. This type of anxiety is often diagnosed as an anxiety disorder (of which there are many), and unfortunately, this type of anxiety often significantly affects a person's behaviours, emotions and thinking patterns. Unlike milder anxiety which sits on the lower end of the spectrum and which usually passes once the stressful event is over; higher levels of anxiety and the accompanying symptoms aren't as easy to shake off and often leaves a person feeling disconnected from others and the world around them whilst savagely trying to fight off constant feelings of constant feelings of threat and dread. Often, anxiety makes a person feel like they are in a constant vicious cycle of threatening thoughts, which in turn affects feelings, which then affects behaviour. Eventually, a person feels worn out, demoralized and above all, very anxious.

For more information on anxiety, the causes and the symptoms, you can visit https://www.mind.org.uk/information-support/types-of-mental-health-problems/anxiety-and-panic-attacks/about-anxiety/

What Are The Symptoms?

These heightened responses within our bodies are regulated by our sympathetic nervous system and by hormones like adrenaline, noradrenalin and cortisol which are released into our blood stream. The process is swift and occurs all by itself – it's not something we are conscious of, and although we can take steps to minimise the unpleasant effects in our bodies, very often it has already kicked in before we can stop it in its tracks. Thankfully, there is a solution and there is help out there in the form of medication and various talking therapies. Whilst I'm not a trained professional, if you are sitting here reading this and can identify, I urge you to seek help, because there is most definitely help out there for you.

Physical symptoms

- Butterflies.
- feeling dizzy or light-headed.
- pins and needles in your hands and feet.
- feeling unable to relax or sit still.
- aches and pains, including tension headaches.

- faster, shallow breathing.
- a fast heartbeat/palpitations.
- excessive sweating.
- sleep problems.
- feeling sick.
- frequent trips to the loo.

Psychological effects

- feeling like you can't relax or can't sit still.
- having a feeling like something bad is about to happen/dread.
- feeling paranoid as though everyone knows you're feeling anxious and feeling like everyone is looking at you.
- worrying that if you stop worrying something bad is going to happen/feeling like worrying is in some way protecting you.
- worrying about losing control or having a panic attack.
- feeling the need to seek reassurance or worried that people are upset or angry with you.
- going over and over situations in your head, ruminating about bad experiences.
- feeling disconnected from your body and mind, as though you are watching someone else. This is known as depersonalisation and is a type of dissociation.
- feeling disconnected from your reality and surroundings, like the world around you isn't real.

This is known as derealisation and is also a type of dissociation.

- excessively worrying about the future and what might happen in the future.

Adult vs Child Anxiety: What Is The Difference?

I'm aware that many of you reading this book will be parents, so I thought it important to address the key differences between adult and child anxiety, as I myself am unlucky enough to have experienced both.

The main thing with child anxiety is that children aren't able to process things around them as easily as adults, simply because their cognitive functioning hasn't yet reached maturity. In other words, their brains aren't fully developed. This means that children identify and respond differently to potential threats and they often can't recognise when their fear reactions have become irrational or intrusive. Children can only go by what and how they are feeling, and very often, unrecognised anxiety in children can display as a child displaying extreme shyness or sensitivity, may be slower to process information, or may be just plain 'acting out'. Let's be clear here though, just because a child is shy or misbehaving doesn't necessarily mean they have anxiety, there are many reasons why this could happen, many of which are a completely normal part of development.

For me personally though, in my early years at school, I was extremely sensitive and withdrawn, and I went through a phase of bursting into tears during class for seemingly no reason. I remember being in primary four at this time, which would have made me about eight years old. These outbursts at school are what eventually led my grandparents to seek professional help for me, although unfortunately at that time my class teacher had no idea how to cope, and simply labelled me as a problem child. In his ignorance, he would tell the other children just to ignore me if I was upset, and on occasion I would be made stand in solitude facing a wall whilst he taught the other children.

In addition to children lacking the ability to verbalise their anxiety, the symptoms of an anxiety disorder can differ to those in adults. Anxiety in a child can incorporate many different symptoms, including:

- Frequent nightmares and disturbed sleep.
- Constant restlessness.
- Sleepiness or falling asleep in school.
- Difficulty concentrating.
- Irritability.
- Crying, tantrums.

As someone who has suffered from both adult and childhood anxiety, I have found that the main 'fight, fright or freeze' symptoms have remained more or less the same, however it's the content of my worries that have changed over the years.

When I was a child, my biggest fear was being abandoned. I remember being worried whether or not my grandparents would decide to come and collect me from school each day, and I remember frequently making excuses not to go to friends' houses or birthday parties, because I was scared that nobody would come and collect me. Nothing gran or papa did or said could reassure me back then, and to their credit, although they encouraged me to step out of my comfort zone and actively sought opportunities for me to do so, I was never forced to do something I was deeply uncomfortable with. Looking back, I can see just how much my grandparents worked together in helping me overcome anxiety. They helped me through creating stability and routine in my life, which cultivated a circle of trust between all of us. Life became predictable in a comforting way which meant that as I got older and started to recover, I gradually began to feel more confident in stepping out of my comfort zone, be it visiting a friend's house or attending a birthday party, trusting that gran and papa would always be there to collect me, or at least be at the end of a phone if I needed them.

Looking back, it must have been a really difficult time for my grandparents. At a time when most people's children have flown the nest and with retirement looming, many couples must feel finally free to pursue their dreams and spending the time they put aside for their family in their youth re-discovering each other, their passions and so forth. Contrast this with my grandparents who had not only become parents again; they were having to cope with a highly sensitive and anxious child who relied upon them for everything. Never once did my grandparents complain or make me feel unwanted, it was actually the total opposite. I was made to feel cherished, celebrated and accepted, even with my crippling anxiety. My grandparents would tell me I was the best thing that had happened to them. How fortunate

I feel now to have had them tell me how wanted and loved I was.

As I got older, my worries matured and I suppose it wasn't completely irrational to worry about my grand-parents' age and health, however the idea of them dying was an unhealthy preoccupation I had for many years, and a nightmare I'd have on a regular basis. Into the bargain, being brought up by my grandparents meant growing up around a much older generation. While my friends' parents were in their thirties and forties, my grandparents became my parents in their sixties, meaning I was always surrounded by much older people, especially as I reached my teens. Papa came from a large family with many siblings, and gran had two other siblings, both of whom passed away when I was in my teens, and both of whom I was very close with. It was hard to remind myself that the people I considered to be my aunts and uncles were actually my great-aunts and great-uncles; cousins were often second cousins, and I can't remember how many trips we made to the hospital to visit very sick relatives. By the time I was sixteen, I'd never been to a wedding, but had attended countless funerals, including my own father's. It sounds silly, and I can have a laugh about it but it actually turned me into a total hypochondriac; although therapy has made me realise that worrying about my own health isn't really surprising given all I've witnessed in my own relatively short lifespan.

Why Me?

Gran and papa were dad's parents. I first came to live with 'gran and papa' when I was a few months old and this continued off and on until my dad received full custody of me when I was around three. From this age until around ten, I would visit mum and my other granny (whom I'll call 'Granny T') once a month at weekends. Up until dad gained full custody of me when I was around three, I could be living with gran and papa for weeks, even months at a time, and out of the blue they would get a call from mum wanting me back. And they'd have to take me back. I remember clinging to my gran, screaming for her not to leave me, and mum gently prizing me out of her arms.

Before I go any further, I know how this sounds. You're probably wondering why my grandparents had me in the first place, why mum let me go, and why she wanted me back. I want to explain that my mother is not a bad person. It took me many years (well into adulthood) to understand, but I now realise that mum had been battling her own demons throughout her life. As a child, I found her scary and unpredictable. At the same time, she was brilliant, beautiful and funny. I just wasn't ever sure which person I was going to get from one visit to the next. As a teenager, we lost touch, or rather, I hit seventeen and disowned her. If anyone asked me where my mum was, I would always mention something vague about her having a drink problem and that we weren't in touch.

I suppose the most reasonable explanation for my living with my grandparents is that mum and dad just couldn't look after me. Yes, they loved me, but they were selfish, mixed up and young. They wanted to drink, socialise and escape their responsibilities. I don't even think they wanted to be together – safe to say, I wasn't planned. Whilst there are so many amazing young mums and dads out there who rise to the challenge of becoming parents, unfortunately parenthood just wasn't achievable for mine, as each of them had their own personal problems and struggles. From what I gather, mum had a tough upbringing with three much older siblings, a premenopausal mother and elderly father who had made it clear to her she wasn't wanted. She had experienced trauma at a young age, although I'm not sure exactly what.

My dad had loving parents and a stable upbringing, but from what I understand, he was painfully shy as a child and had inner struggles with confidence. Although it has never been confirmed, there is no doubt in my mind that dad was an anxiety sufferer and it was never fully recognised until it was too late. Ultimately, this resulted in the two of my parents becoming alcoholics.

Mum and dad did try to make things work for my sake. Dad, who was then an apprentice engineer with Rolls Royce, quit his job and proposed to mum. She turned him down. We all moved to Kent briefly to stay with my mum's older sister, Liz and her then husband. Dad tried to find work, and mum and Liz between them looked after me. In short, things didn't work out, and my parents moved back to Scotland with me in tow. Money was tight, and they both liked to drink. Fights and arguments broke out. I'm quite a passionate, fiery person at times and I think I have both of my parents to thank for that. For the two of them though, it was like a clash of titans. Mum would go out and not come back for days. Dad had his own problems with alcohol, although at that time, from what I gather he wasn't as troubled as mum.

Years later, dad needed to go into the hospital to get his nose fixed as it had been badly broken in the past. I remember asking how he had broken his nose and after some coaxing he told me that one night he had been sleeping in the living room at his and mum's house. They were no longer together but he was still living with us to look after me. I was sleeping beside him as a baby. When mum returned from a night out, she had brought a man back with her. He had taken a look at my dad sleeping and kicked him repeatedly in the face, breaking his nose. Another time, I remember being in mum's arms and them fighting (no doubt, alcohol fuelled), and dad pushing my mum whilst I was in her arms and I remember being scared she was going to drop me. I think dad hit mum once when he was drunk. He was no angel, neither of them were. Once, mum dragged her nails all the way down dad's face and left him badly bleeding.

As I said before, dad was no angel, nor did he pretend to be. What I will say though is that not once did I ever see him falling around drunk. I remember occasionally smelling it on his breath but would think nothing of it as many young guys go down the pub for a couple of pints. Sometimes I would hear gran arguing with him on the phone, but on the whole everyone's relationship seemed pretty good back then. It was actually a surprise when I was around twelve and dad was telling me he was going to AA meetings. I remember wondering why, and then realising quickly what he had been trying to hide for a long time, as for any of you who have ever experienced addiction or know anyone who has, withdrawal and recovery is one of the most gruelling journeys anyone will ever face. It's also a terrible time for families.

When dad gave up alcohol, he would never be quite the same as he was before. It had done something to his brain, broken it beyond repair. He was never able to hold down a job; he was often paranoid and developed an inferiority complex. He became obsessed with guitar and the only way I can describe it is he became a total hippie. I know it sounds funny, and I'm smiling to myself as I write it, but whilst it was okay for a while, he just got weirder and weirder and had all these weird friends, until eventually he stopped visiting so much (when I was around fourteen) and when he did visit, he was dopey and would fall asleep mid-sentence. Thankfully, my life at that point revolved around music school, my friends, my violin and my grandparents, and all of this really helped to cushion what was happening with my dad.

Anyway, I remember a full-blown argument between my grandparents and my dad one evening when he came to us for dinner. Papa was basically accusing my dad of "being 'on' something" and dad was emphatically denying it. I remember gran pleading with him that it wasn't good for me, his daughter, to be seeing him this way, and that he needed help and they wanted to help. He retorted, "well, in that case I just won't be able to come and visit because there's nothing wrong with me, you are the ones with the problem." I remember papa responding with, "well, don't come back until you've sorted yourself out". At that, dad got up and stormed out.

That was the last time I ever saw my dad, as a few weeks later I would be taken into the school office by two police officers, who told me dad had taken his own life.

I should mention that dad lived with my grandparents until I was about six, when he got his own house. I had the option to go and stay with him but by that time I was so settled with my grandparents and wanted to stay with them. It didn't make much of a difference to me as dad was always around and showed me much love and affection. It's so sad what addiction does to people, because like my mum, alcohol truly changed his personality and ultimately, determined his fate. Gran would often confide in me how powerless she had felt, how she had failed him in some way, and how she didn't know what had happened to him.

Gran and papa, who had three sons, doted on my dad. He was the middle child, and my grandparents would proudly tell me stories of him growing up, each of them beaming at one another. As a child, I was told he was a 'good' baby, never fussy. As an infant he wouldn't leave my gran's side, and would often hide behind her, clinging onto her skirt if faced with anyone he wasn't familiar with. He was a shy and pensive child, whom, in his early years at school would often save some of his cake or biscuit at lunchtime, wrap it carefully in a napkin and take it home for his mum. As he got older, he was a keen footballer who showed real promise, having inherited his dad's talent for the sport. School reports were encouraging, although it was clear dad was always a bit of a dreamer as a teacher had pointed out that he tended to be 'giddy' at times. Whilst his older brother, David, was going off the rails as a teen, drinking and causing embarrassment for his parents, my dad who was only a couple of years younger would solemnly swear to his mother that he would never turn out like his brother.

Unfortunately, none of this lasted, and it would later transpire that dad detested his school years, especially high school. Back then, it was the seventies and rebellion was in the air. Dad would frequently play truant and soon his dreams of becoming a footballer would dissipate. He fell in with the wrong crowd, discovering girls, booze and rebellion. I'd like to say 'the rest is history', but it was just the beginning of a downward spiral for dad.

Looking back to my own childhood, I'm pretty sure it was after the nose-breaking incident that dad decided enough was enough. He gathered what he could, and left, taking me to live with his parents. That night, dad and I had arrived at gran and papa's with what little belongings we had. It was too late for regular shops to be open, so papa drove us all to an overnight pharmacy, where they bought powdered milk, nappies and other baby essentials. From there, it should have been plain sailing, but a few weeks later, mum wanted me back.

And as I say, this pattern of being between houses continued until I was around three, when dad gained full custody, and my grandparents became my guardians.

Eventually, mum moved in with her mother, 'Granny T' and once a month, I would visit them both. Granny T and I had a lot of fun, and she was very good to me, with seemingly boundless energy despite her advancing years. Mum had become involved with a guy who lived in the next block of flats to my granny. He seemed nice enough, but I can't remember him much, other than mum lived with him for a while and appeared besotted with him. I would sometimes visit his and mum's flat while I was visiting Granny T, and honestly, it was always rather a pleasant environment. Sadly it didn't last long, as from what I can remember, he ended up going to prison for assaulting someone. Mum was heartbroken and moved back in with Granny T.

Poor mum, how I feel for her now. Like my dad, she was intelligent, creative, witty, funny, full of such potential. Sadly, trauma in her younger years would change the course of her life, and she became a really mixed up person. If she had been drinking when I visited, she would often ramble. I don't think she meant to, or even realised it, but back then she terrified me. She also seemed to hate my gran (dad's mum) back then, and would make up stories about her. This really, really hurt, as I loved my gran beyond measure. Looking back, I see it's because mum wanted to give me all the things gran did - the things she wasn't able to give me at that time.

It took me such a long time to realise that mum was a victim, and just because someone's behaviour displays as one thing, no one has any idea what could be going on behind the scenes within that person's life, or what trauma they have experienced in the past. I now see that when I would visit as a child, mum's ramblings were those of a deeply wounded, traumatised person. Aside from a difficult childhood, I fear she experienced unimaginable abuse and was taken advantage of as a young and vulnerable woman.

As an adult myself, I realise now that mum was trying to protect me in the only way she could convey. When she had been drinking, she would try to warn me about the potential dangers in the world. She didn't realise I was too young to be warned of rape or to be told in depth about periods, sex, drugs and what happened to a baby when it was aborted. Had I been older, my brain may have been mature enough to process what I was being told, but as an innocent child, I was scared, confused and disturbed.

It got to the point where I dreaded visiting mum and Granny T. My grandparents knew that mum would sometimes be drinking whilst I was there, but they had to put their trust in her and Granny T, because mum had every right to see me, and who were they to stop that? You have to remember, I was five or six at this time, maybe even younger, so it wouldn't be until a few years later, with the help of a child psychologist that I would eventually be able to articulate and verbalise to my grandparents the scary thoughts and ideas mum was unintentionally filling my head with. It wouldn't be until I was about seven or eight that the emotional damage would become visible, so whilst I could see it pained her, gran would coax me to go, explaining how mum really wanted to see me and that I would have a great time once I was there.

Sometimes I would go to visit and it would just be Granny T and I, and my mum wouldn't be there. Eventually that became a relief, but in the younger years, I would be eagerly waiting for her to arrive, and sometimes she did. Other times, I would go a weekend without seeing her. I remember a couple of occasions where mum didn't arrive, and I wanted to see her so badly that Granny T let me walk over to the next block of flats, and ring the buzzer of mum's boyfriend to find out if she was there. Sometimes she was, and sometimes she wasn't.

Granny T was a lovely granny and very kind to me. I remember us being silly together, and her playing with me tirelessly whilst I was there visiting. However I remember Sunday mornings being a bit of an ordeal, as it was Granny T's day out to lunch with some friends who lived nearby. I would either have my gran and papa pick me up early, or if mum was there, I would have to stay with her until they arrived. I always dreaded those Sunday mornings. It was okay when mum hadn't been drinking, but if she had, I would beg my Granny T not to leave me. I'm not sure if Granny T realised just how anxious I felt, she probably knew that my grandparents would be coming to collect me shortly and maybe thought I was overreacting, but what I do remember is begging her not to leave me and she always did.

The main thing I remember was feeling so powerless, and ultimately the overwhelming feeling of relief that would wash over me when I eventually saw my grandparents' car appear outside the entrance below. This meant I could finally go home and not have to worry about any of it for another month.

As I've gotten older, I've come to accept my mum for who she is. Although I haven't physically seen her in over twelve years, we are in brief contact. Mum has been sober for nearly two years now. She lives alone with her cat, Lola. In the twelve years since I've seen her, her life has been a rollercoaster of events. Nevertheless, she has remained strong and overcome traumas no one should ever have to experience. For this, I admire her and I'm proud that she is sober and becoming stronger each day. I am pleased that she continues to rebuild her life.

Childhood Therapy

Things changed when I started seeing a child psychologist called Claire. Eventually, it got to the point where visits to Granny T became so stressful for me that my grandparents were told by Claire not to let me visit without my gran physically being there with me. Granny T and my gran got along well enough, but it could be tricky with my mum, as she always blamed my gran for taking over. By that time though, it had become clear that I needed some sort of psychological help, and ultimately everyone pulled together to help me as best they could. My schoolwork was suffering, and I was becoming withdrawn and constantly upset in class. My little brain was so saturated by the information given to it by the time I was eight, that I had become fearful of virtually everything, including eating.

In mum's ramblings over the years, she had warned me to stay away from policemen because they would take your fingerprints and put you in jail, so I became terrified of authority figures, especially policemen. I also saw an episode of The Bill once (police drama) and it showed fictional CCTV footage of criminals, which now I can see is quite funny, but back then, from that moment I became obsessed with cameras and was terrified someone watching me wherever I went.

Any advert or TV programme, no matter how seemingly innocent, had the potential to send me into an anxiety-fuelled tailspin. Once I saw a programme on morning television as I ate my breakfast, detailing the consequences of drug smuggling in airports. It showed a man sitting on the floor of a prison cell all-alone, surrounded by nothing but grey walls. He looked so lonely! After seeing that advert and imagining how awful it must feel to be stuck in a prison cell, I became preoccupied with the idea that someone had somehow planted drugs in my pockets or bag, and I too would get accused of carrying drugs. I must have been really young because I remember this particular fear spilled over into one visit I had with Granny T. I remember her taking me to the Transport Museum in Glasgow and us visiting the gift shop there. I had a little purse that my gran and papa had given me for my visit, which I clutched to proudly. I remember standing in the shop browsing through the bits and bobs whilst Granny T was in another part of the shop looking at something else. Suddenly out of nowhere, an idea came to me that I somehow had drugs in my purse. In a blind panic, I tried to reason with my own self that there was no possible way there could be. Still, anxiety persevered, and told me otherwise. I began to sweat and started to feel the room spinning. Granny T was around the corner, totally oblivious to the internal panic attack I was having. I panicked further, as in my innocence, I thought that I wouldn't even be able to check my purse, because what if I opened it and people would think I was stealing something? After all, I had already clocked the CCTV when we walked in.

I can't remember what happened after that, but at some point I managed to find Granny T and we went home together. I never told Granny T what happened earlier that day, as back then I didn't even know how to verbalise how I was feeling, and in any case, I was sure she wouldn't understand. Even at this young age, I somehow knew it was all in my head, and I was worried if I told anyone they would want to lock me away somewhere and throw away the key. Only my gran knew and understood my deepest fears. Ultimately, I remember calling her whilst Granny T was in the other room and sobbing down the phone that I was scared that my hands were dirty, and I had drugs on them. I remember gran's distress on the other line, insisting that she come to get me, but I plead with her not to as I didn't want a fuss, and I didn't want to tell Granny T, who was pottering away in the other room. I could hear the anguish in gran's voice as over the phone, she told me in a gentle voice to put my hands to the receiver so she could kiss them, telling me I had lovely little clean hands and that everything was going to be just fine.

Meanwhile...

Somewhere in the middle of all of this, dad had begun a relationship with a woman called Steph from our village. Steph had a little boy called Alfie who, at that time, was around two or three. Dad was around fourteen years Steph's senior, but that didn't seem to matter and at that time they both seemed happy enough. I had enough on my plate back then with school, anxiety and my mum, so I don't have any vivid memories of their relationship, other than that Steph was nice to me and always seemed to be at dad's house whenever I visited. By that point, dad had his own place, and although I was given the choice to go with him, I decided to remain with my grandparents. Apparently, he was still drinking heavily back then, despite the fact I never actually saw him drunk, that for which I am thankful.

Anyway, the next thing was that dad had moved in with Steph and they were having a baby. I remember the night dad told gran. Let's just say she wasn't exactly overjoyed with the news, given everything else that was going on. I remember the atmosphere in the house and dad taking me into my room and me crying as he was telling me. It's hard to admit, but I couldn't help but feel betrayed, and I was a real 'daddy's girl'. Nevertheless, I loved babies, and I was going to be a big sister; it couldn't be all that bad, surely?

~❖~

My sister Jenna was born, and it was love at first sight. I remember holding her in my arms and thinking how tiny and perfect she looked. Unfortunately though, dad and Steph were on the rocks. Their situation wasn't too dissimilar to my own parents in that they both drank heavily, and sadly their relationship went downhill not long after Jenna was born. Dad eventually moved back into his old place, where he had allowed his brother David to stay whilst he was living with Steph. For a short period, dad and David lived together, although they had never gotten along, and it wasn't long before David found his own place and dad was living on his own again.

After that, things seemed to be calm and 'normal' for a while. Dad stopped drinking and smoking; he took up yoga and the guitar and as I mentioned, began to make friends with a bunch of hippies. Although he would never be the same as he was when I was little, I was so proud of who he was becoming and of his inner strength in battling addiction. The fact that he had a shorter fuse than normal or tended to be paranoid a lot of the time didn't matter to me; he was my dad and I loved him, and that was that.

Throughout this time, I remained with my grandparents, which was more than fine with me. Neither of them drank nor smoked, and they were devout Catholics; so aside from being back and forth at my mum's once a month and dad having a baby with Steph, life with my grandparents overall was blissfully calm. My grandparents were all 'mine', and I was all theirs. I never saw them as grandparents; they were my parents and they treated me as their daughter. As I continued to grow and mature, their love for me remained unconditional, and they were never slow to tell me how much I changed their lives and how proud they were of me. Gran described me as the 'daughter she never had' and God help anyone who papa met on the street, as he would often drag them inside and play them one of the many violin recordings I had made 'just for him'.

I wanted for absolutely nothing. They took me everywhere with them, dressed me in the very best and we went on holidays three times a year. They honestly couldn't have done more for me; I was cherished, championed, accepted, nurtured, considered, valued. It was everything a child could ask for and more, and that love, nurture and support ultimately changed the course of my life for the better.

Looking back through my earliest memories, I suppose it isn't really surprising that I developed anxiety as early on as I did. There was a lot of toing and froing for me as a child, and a lot of uncertainty over where I would be living and with whom. It's also completely plausible that my anxiety is genetic, as mental illness runs on both sides of my family.

The three or four years I spent with dad before he passed were probably the best our relationship had ever seen. He would take me out to the cinema every Friday night. We would get dressed up and go on little 'dates', and he would take me to music concerts and he tried to teach me the guitar. When I was struggling with maths at school, he came and sat with me, explaining everything patiently. It's funny because he was so impatient with silly things like waiting in queues, or being in large crowds, yet so extremely patient with other things, like teaching me how to do things.

He was good at maths, being an engineer. Not once did he become impatient with me, and he made it clear that he had all the time in the world for me. He was proud of me, and I was proud of him. We looked so alike. Our personalities were very similar, as was our morbid sense of humour. I knew I could tell dad anything and he wouldn't judge me; in fact, he told me this himself once as he was teaching me how to drive his red Ford Mondeo around the local business park one night (when I was fourteen!)

Dad was a sensitive and intuitive person. If I'm being honest, I try not to think about him too much because it hurts remembering how alike we were, especially now that I'm older and can see things I couldn't see before. Sometimes I worry that dad thought I didn't need him because I had papa. I really hope this wasn't true, because he couldn't have been more wrong. Dad understood me when no one else could, because I was an extension of him.

Sadly, herein lies the tragedy of suicide. For those left behind, it's devastating to know that you will never receive answers to the questions you need answered so desperately by that person. Questions such as why they did it, did they know how loved they were; and thoughts that if only I had been there, if only he had called me. Dad's death simultaneously tore the whole family apart whilst bringing my grandparents and myself closer together, forming an ever-impenetrable bond. In the years following dad's death, papa could never utter his name, and gran couldn't talk about him without crying.

Dad was fiercely proud to a fault, so would literally deny any wrongdoing to the death. Ultimately, dad was pulled over by the police for driving under the influence of Valium, and it later transpired that the police also found the car littered with the little blue pills. The shame was all too much to bear for dad, especially after vehemently denying any wrongdoing to gran and papa's face. Dad would later state in a suicide note that he was a coward, and that he would always be with me whenever I played music, and to tell his beautiful daughter Jenna, that he loved her.

Gran and I often reminisced together about dad, quickly changing the subject if ever papa came into the room. For papa, the memories of dad were too painful to bear, but gran and I needed to talk about him, to remember him for who he was, not for who he ultimately became.

Fifteen was a pretty bleak year for me, and it would have been all too easy to have gone off the rails. Thankfully, I had the unwavering support of my grandparents, along with the distraction of school deadlines, music, the violin and my friends. I quickly realised that things would never be the same following dad's death, and for years to come, I would often feel a sense of un-balance. For those who have experienced the loss of a loved one, you may strongly identify with this feeling. For those who have never experienced it, the best way I can describe it is to imagine you have recently lost a limb.

Let's say it's your right arm. You have been so used to it always being there that you kind of took it for granted. Suddenly it's not there anymore, but you can't accept it because the memory and sensation of it being there is so vivid. It even gets itchy sometimes, but when you absentmindedly reach over to scratch it, you re-live the horror and memory that it's no longer there anymore, and you're left feeling off-balance and confused all over again.

Although the feeling of loss and grief never really goes away, time and life eventually gets in the way, and helps to distract you. Over time, you learn to live with that loss and grief, eventually accepting it as a part of you. You never forget that person, and somewhere deep within you, a special place is reserved in your heart for the memories you shared with them. A lot of the time, especially in the early days, it's too painful to dig deep to retrieve those memories you have so painstakingly buried, but sometimes in your own quiet moments, you choose to reach in and take them out one at a time, just to have a little look and spend a little time - not too much, though, as it might open a Pandora's Box of pain and suffering. Quietly and carefully, you place each memory back in its little box and lock each memory away safely for another time.

School Days Are The Happiest Days Of Your Life

In Scotland, the primary school system starts at primary one, which begins between the ages four-and-a-half to five, and goes through to primary seven, between ages eleven and twelve. As my birthday is in February, my grandparents had the option of either sending me to school at four-and-a-half which would mean I would be one of the youngest in my class, or to wait until the following year when I would turn five, which was the advice given by the nursery staff at the time.

The main issue for my grandparents though was that my nursery was in Clydebank, which was a good four miles away from where we lived,

whereas the local primary school was a five-minute walk away, and because of the instability I had faced in the early years, my grandparents were keen for me to begin primary school as soon as possible. In retrospect, we all agreed that I probably wasn't ready to start school when I did, but nevertheless it was important for my grandparents to enrol me at school locally to establish some sort of normality within our hectic lives at that time.

Despite being the youngest in my class and painfully shy, I coped fairly well between the years of primary one to three. I think my grandparents were so relieved that I seemed to be settling in well, however their relief would be short-lived, as the first half of primary four was when my own personal nightmare with anxiety began. Any little fuss I caused in the first three years at primary school, I made up for tenfold in the first half of the fourth. How did this present itself in my feelings and behaviour? Well, my thoughts would race and I wouldn't be able to breathe. I'd unsuspectingly be sitting in class, and all of a sudden a frightening thought would cross my mind, and there I was, suddenly bursting into tears for what would appear to be no reason whatsoever.

Primary four is the year I remember most vividly for being both the best and worst year of my life. I was eight and I had found myself in a boisterous composite class of primary threes and primary fours. My childhood memory of the teacher was that he was a large brute of a man, who seemingly towered over us all with beads of sweat running uncontrollably down his bald bulbous head, his face often puce at the sheer effort of trying to control the class. He wore distinctively intense cologne that you could smell on approach to his classroom, and you could often hear his thunderous voice reverberating all the way down the corridor when he shouted, which he seemed to do a lot. Needless to say, the man utterly terrified me. He also had no time for a

bottom for maths. In fact, my friends and I would have such a laugh at how bad I was at maths.

So, back to primary four. In my mind, the only thing that year really had going for it was that it was common knowledge that this was the year children would be selected to play the violin through an audition process. Given that I had wanted to play from the moment I set eyes on the older girls with their violin cases, and also that I was the child who was obsessed with musicals, when the time came for the school's violin teacher, Mrs Alves, to come around the classes with her notepad asking for a show of hands of who might be interested in auditioning for the violin, my hand instantly shot up, along with six others much to my dismay.

For about a week before the audition, I couldn't sleep, as I knew that only two children out of the whole year group would be chosen, and I was worried I wouldn't be one of them. I would lie in bed imagining being handed my very own violin in its case, and how I would proudly walk around school carrying it. I hoped and prayed that I would be chosen, knowing in my heart it was something that just I had to do.

Finally, the day of the audition arrived, and the soft-spoken Mrs Alves ushered our group into a little room I'd never been in before. Inside the room stood an upright piano, along with six little chairs, which had been arranged in a semi-circle. Mrs Alves indicated for us all to sit down. Not knowing what to expect, I remember the six of us looking from one to the other, wondering what was coming next. After the initial introductions were out of the way, I remember the murmurs of surprise from the group as Mrs Alves explained that she was going to play the 'Happy Birthday' melody (not the Stevie Wonder version) on the piano. She then explained that she was going to go around the group and we were to each take a turn of singing the melody along with her piano accompaniment. I remember us all giggling, finding the notion funny and peculiar, but singing the well-known song quickly put us all at ease.

As a violin teacher now, I understand the reasoning behind why Mrs Alves had asked us to sing 'Happy Birthday' that day. Aside from the fact that virtually everyone knows the melody and words, it's actually a notoriously difficult song to sing in tune, as it requires the singer to begin the melody at an appropriate pitch in order to reach the octave (seven note leap) in the final line. The part that goes, "Happy biiiirthday, dear ....." is the most challenging part, especially if from the outset, the singer has begun at the top end of their range of pitch, thus setting themselves up for failure in the last line...

This friendly but fiendish little song is perfect for music teachers and can be used universally with students to determine ability in pitch and aural awareness in the initial lessons.

Much to my delight, I was chosen to play the violin, along with a studious, sweet girl from the other class called 'Mia'. Mia and I would attend lessons every Wednesday for half an hour after school, and Wednesdays quickly became my favourite day of the week. Violin lessons would always pass too quickly, and I remember having such a thirst for information; I just couldn't get enough. I remember being given my first ever violin to take home. I couldn't get home quickly enough to show it to my grandparents. I remember that battered little case with the green felting, cocooning the small violin nestled inside. It was love at first sight. I coveted that little violin, and often opened the case just to marvel at its beauty. I dedicated a special corner of my room for it to sit safely and I would frequently gaze over at it as I dosed off to sleep, imagining all the adventures we would have together. The violin soon became my best friend, and as I would later find out, a one-way ticket to a better life.

Not long after beginning lessons, Mia moved away to another school and was replaced by another girl named 'Gail'. After a month or so, Gail decided she didn't want to play the violin, so that left just myself and Mrs Alves, whom, much to my delight, decided she would continue to teach me privately.

This was when my playing really started improving, along with my confidence.

I had gone from being a little girl who was afraid of virtually everything to having finally found something of my very own that I adored and was proud of. The sessions with psychologist Claire were finally paying off, and although I wasn't completely out of the woods with anxiety, my schoolwork and concentration had improved exponentially. Primary four was finally coming to an end, and I would soon be entering into primary five as a much happier child.

Sessions with Claire, along with my violin lessons, left my mind clear and virtually free from worry, which meant I had a greater capacity for learning and a sudden thirst for all things violin-related.

By the time I entered into primary five, I had already sat my first graded exam on the violin, which was a year earlier than the other pupils at school. I remember visiting our local high school to sit the exam along with a group of violinists from the year above. Normally, this type of outing would have sent me into a whirlwind of anxiety, but thanks to my new sense of self-confidence, the only nerves I really felt that day were directed towards the exam itself.

The exam turned out to be a great success, and afterwards my gran, who had accompanied me there, told me that as she had been standing outside the exam room listening to me play, the head of music had been passing and had stopped to listen. He had asked her how old I was, and when she told him he was surprised and said he assumed I had been older given my ability. He said he couldn't wait to teach me when I eventually came to high school.

When the certificates were presented out one morning at our school assembly, to my delight I had been the only pupil awarded with a distinction. What's more, much to my embarrassment (and secret pleasure), the head teacher at our school had framed our certificates in the main foyer of the school for everyone to see as they entered and exited the building.

Meanwhile, although my parents were still very much dealing with their own problems, my home life with gran and papa continued to be stable and nurturing. Gran and Papa, who were thrilled that their timid granddaughter had finally found her feet, strongly encouraged my passion for the violin and helped in every way they could. One day in particular, they surprised me with a trip to the music shop and allowed me to pick my very own violin.

Saturday visits to the local music shop became a frequent occurrence, and papa would patiently wait outside in the car for what probably felt to him like hours, while myself and gran would excitedly sift through the stacks of books the music shop had to offer. It is no exaggeration to say that each week, I'd come away with bundles of music books, usually of repertoire much too advanced for me at the time, and gran would arrange for any books that were not available in store, to be sent to our home directly.

Once at home, I would devour the books. I remember attending my lessons each week, asking to play different pieces of music, and my violin teacher happily agreeing to teach me whichever piece I'd set my heart on. There was still so much to learn, but back then I couldn't have been happier. Mrs Alves' lessons were calm, fun and inspiring. She made me feel relaxed and safe, and my grandparents were eternally grateful for everything she was continuing to do for me.

Although anxiety would still come and go, my frequent sessions with psychologist Claire were helping me to manage and understand my fears, whilst learning the violin was helping to challenge them. A good example was when I had to visit a larger primary school a few miles away for a local youth orchestra that Mrs Alves coaxed me into attending. The very first year I attended, I was one of the youngest players, and had happily found myself sitting at the back of the second violins where I could remain practically invisible. I remember there being a big concert at the end of our rehearsals, where everyone's parents came watch, but other than this, I don't remember much else about it.

The second year I can remember in a bit more detail. The rehearsals were in the summer term of the school year for an evening a week for a couple of hours. I remember that whilst everyone else's parents would leave and come back to collect them after rehearsals, I wasn't about to let my grandparents off the hook that easily. I was scared that if they left, they wouldn't come back, so to ensure that I actually went to the rehearsals without having a flaky midway through, gran and papa waited out in the car for the duration of each rehearsal. When it came time to have our break halfway through, I would sneak off to the toilets, where I knew there was a good view of the school car park, and peer out of the window making sure they hadn't left. As always, our trusty red Passat would be sitting there, waiting for me to finish rehearsing. As I got a bit older and overcame anxiety, we would all have a good chuckle at the idea of all of this, but back then, my grandparents were willing to help their anxious granddaughter overcome her mental health obstacles in any way they could. Writing this, I'm having a giggle to myself, but my heart is also bursting with pride and love for my selfless grandparents, who completely put their own lives to one side for me. I don't know many parents who would go to that extent, let alone grandparents.

Okay, so now comes a part where I'm feeling a bit sorry for my younger self as I write this, but I'm also having a giggle too. So, the evening of the concert had finally arrived. As I mentioned, it was my second year taking part in this orchestra, although this year I had been told to sit right at the front of the orchestra, beside the adult waving a stick, having not a clue why I was being asked to do so. At least I had a better view, I thought to myself, smiling ignorantly up at the wizard-like figure (who I'd later learn was called the "conductor").

When it came to the evening of the concert, much to my confusion, I had been asked to hold back and wait until the rest of the orchestra were seated before walking onto the stage on my own. I had absolutely zero idea why this was, but obediently complied without question. I remember being given a round of applause on approach to my chair, adding further to my perplexity, but I smiled anyway and focused on the main task at hand, which was to scan the crowd in search of my grandparents. After a brief moment of panic where I couldn't find them, my eyes eventually fell on my gran's white hair. Phew, they were here. Now I could relax!

At the interval, papa asked me why I had walked onto the stage on my own, and I confessed to being puzzled too, and told him I had no idea. It wasn't until after the concert that another parent approached me and congratulated me on being a fantastic leader. Later, the penny would drop and I would realise that the reason I was being made a fuss over was because I had been leading the orchestra the whole time, and it was customary for the leader of the orchestra to enter onto the stage once the rest of the orchestra was already seated, and at the end of the concert, to exit the stage before the rest of the orchestra. At the time though, I was completely oblivious.

Soon, Mrs Alves would invite me to play in and attend concerts out with the school. She was a member of the Salvation Army and she invited me along one weekend to play for a coffee morning. Another time, she invited me to go and watch her own daughter play in a chamber music ensemble. Her daughter was already an accomplished violinist, and I remember watching in awe as she performed on stage, hoping desperately that maybe one day that could be me.

From what I can remember, primary five was relatively uneventful, not that I was complaining. I was still visiting mum and Granny T once a month, but just on the Friday evening with my gran, as per psychologist Claire's instruction. This turned out to be best all round for everyone and our visits became rather enjoyable, especially when mum was on form and she was the life and soul of the evening, being her zany, colourful, and hilarious self.

In primary six, as my teachers began preparing my friends for attending our local high school, my grandparents began to brooch the idea of my attending a specialist music school. Prospectuses for a nearby music school started to arrive through the post, although I remember shutting the idea down completely at the time. Yes, my anxiety had improved hugely, but that didn't mean I was ready to leave all my friends and go to a whole new school in a different area where I knew no one, not a chance. Into the bargain, there would be a two round audition process for this particular school, one of which involved an overnight stay. I couldn't even imagine it. I wasn't about to be abandoned overnight with a group of people I had never met. No way, I was having none of it. All I wanted to do was fit in with my friends, move on up to high school like everyone else, and live a quiet life, ideally free from anxiety.

In the end though, somehow they all managed to persuade me to audition, and it was mostly down to Mrs Alves and her calming influence. Also, on a few occasions, I had visited Mrs Alves' home for violin lessons. There, she had introduced me to her husband, Peter Alves, who just happened to be the Director of Music at the Music School of Douglas Academy in Milngavie. Mr Alves was a tall, slender man with a gentle charm and warm personality. His kind face and ready smile made me feel at ease the moment I met him. Whilst I was there visiting, Mrs Alves would often call Mr Alves in from the other room to accompany me on piano. It was probably around then, in their beautiful music room, with the comfort of the music, my violin on my shoulder and my gran by my side, that it occurred to me that perhaps things were going to be okay after all and maybe, just maybe, I could imagine myself going to music school.

Auditions

It has been twelve years since I left Douglas Academy, and since then many things have changed, although some have remained the same. Throughout this book, when I refer to my memories of Douglas Academy, it will be as it was whilst I was a pupil there, which was between the years of 2002-2008. Since that time, the building itself has changed, and so has many of the staff, including the Director of Music who retired the year I left, and also the Head Teacher, who I think retired that same year.

Douglas Academy is situated in Milngavie (pronounced Mulguy), which is a town in East Dunbartonshire and a suburb of Glasgow. Milngavie sits on the Allander Water and lies on the edge of the north-west of Greater Glasgow, roughly about ten kilometres from the city centre.

Milngavie is probably best known for its beautiful scenery as it lies at the beginning of the famous West Highland Way, a linear long-distance footpath, which runs from Milngavie northwards for 154 kilometres to the town of Fort William in the Highlands of Scotland. Despite the school being located in the heart of the town of Milngavie, the building itself is nestled within thirty-six acres of the very picturesque Mains Estate, once home to the Douglases of Mains, a branch family of the ancient Clan Douglas, hence the name of the school.

Douglas Academy, which first opened in 1967, is a comprehensive secondary school serving pupils from Milngavie and the surrounding areas, which includes Craigton and Baldernock. The school itself is considered to be one of Scotland's top performing state schools, and each year the school continues to rank amongst the highest in the country.

The Music School of Douglas Academy opened in 1979, and quickly established itself as a national Centre of Excellence. Applications for entry are received each year from all over Scotland, and boarding facilities are provided for pupils who live too far away to commute. The music school is state funded by the Scottish Government and is supported by East Dunbartonshire council.

For pupils within the music school, around 20% of the week is timetabled around musical subjects, with normal academic curriculum for the remainder of the week. Every pupil has a specialist instrumental tutor for their first and second study instruments, who is usually an orchestral player, acclaimed soloist or university lecturer, and tuition is available in all instruments, including voice and composition. The general aim of the school is to cultivate the 'well-rounded' musician, and pupils also take lessons in theory, aural musicianship, history of music, composition, harmony and counterpoint, keyboard musicianship and analysis.

Aside from classroom and instrumental lessons, within the music school, there is a strong emphasis placed on performance, and every opportunity is given to pupils within the school to develop their performance skills both as soloists and within groups.

To be offered a place at the music school of Douglas Academy, you first need to pass two auditions. Whilst I was a pupil there, the school received around thirty-five applications each year. Everyone who applied would be given a first audition, although only around fifteen would be invited back for the second, which took place over two days. The second audition took place at St Andrew's College in Bearsden, a national Roman Catholic teacher-training college, which amalgamated with Glasgow University in 1999 and provided halls of residence for the students there along with the pupils from the music school. Teacher-training eventually relocated to Glasgow in 2002 which meant the building was eventually declared surplus to university requirements, and in 2007, planning permission was granted to construct the new Bearsden Academy which now sits on the former site. Post 2002, the second auditions took part elsewhere, but the year I auditioned, second auditions were still held at the St Andrew's campus.

The second audition was overseen by a small independent group of assessors, whom, throughout the two-day audition process would assess potential candidates in a series of musical activities to determine how they responded to individual and group tutoring sessions.

Mr Alves who was the Director of the music school would often describe music as a language. Language, of course, is a form of communication, and Mr Alves taught his pupils at Douglas that unless a musician was able to play in concert with others and had the ability to respond to a listener, that musical skill and technique didn't count for much at all. This was very much the ethos of the music school, to create a well-rounded musician, and in a sense, the two-day audition process was a simulation of what life would be like as a pupil there.

Following a successful second audition, around twelve pupils would be admitted to the school, regardless of which stage they were at in their secondary education, as Mr Alves didn't believe in a 'catch-all' starting point.

Once it was decided that I would be auditioning for music school, what followed next were a series of open events held at the school for prospective candidates and their parents, which enabled everyone to mingle and to get a real 'feel' for the place.

Having only ever set foot in our local Clydebank High a handful of times, Douglas Academy was unlike any school I'd ever been in before. The first time I visited, it was a bright and crisp winter morning around January. I was with my grandparents, and we were attending the first of many open days.

I remember feeling anticipation mixed with dread as we turned off the main road onto the scenic Craigton Road. Although only a couple of miles long, the drive seemed to go on forever as we drove further along the narrow country road in search of the school, whilst fields emerged and hilltops appeared on the horizon. The anxious voice inside my head began to question how I would be able to cope with this journey each day, because although I wasn't very far from home, this place felt so alien, and so far removed from everything I knew.

This quaint narrow road continued to stretch on for another mile or so until eventually a little white sign reading 'Douglas Academy' appeared with an arrow pointing upwards, towards a concealed narrow incline to the right. Although it couldn't have been far, the road up to the school seemed to stretch on forever as our car gradually ascended the winding path. Once we finally reached the top, we were met with a grassy roundabout upon which sat a neatly cobbled wall with an engraved plaque at the front reading "Douglas Academy" in attractive lettering. As we looked beyond this sign, there, set back from the road lay Douglas Academy. It was a fairly modern building with many windows and blue panelling, which overlooked the stunningly beautiful Campsie fells in the north and the Kilpatrick Hills in the west.

Despite feeling painfully shy on my initial visits to Douglas Academy, I was in no doubt that it was a wonderful place to be. The atmosphere was different there, gentler somehow to any other schools I'd been in.

One of the first things I noticed about the music school in my initial visits was a real sense of camaraderie. Pupils of all ages seemed to be mixing happily with one another, laughing and joking in the music block at break times, whilst the teachers came across as a relaxed, approachable bunch who always seemed genuinely pleased to be there. It was clear that there was a mutual respect between the staff and the pupils, and it was obvious that everyone felt at home there. To me back then, the idea of actually enjoying school was incomprehensible.

If I could try and describe the environment within the music school, I suppose it was less like a school and more like a family. Looking back, this all makes sense, as many pupils from further afield boarded together at the nearby halls of residence. Many had left their families and homes behind from a young age, so pupils and staff pulled together and formed a family in their own right; the halls of residence were literally a 'home-from-home', and staff working in the halls were called 'houseparents'. Houseparents, like real parents, were expected to turn their hands to most things, and played a crucial role in the pupils' development by being ever-present figures amid all the changes you would expect from adolescents. Aside from being expected to juggle teaching and pastoral roles, they were mediators, counsellors, comforters and even cleaners.

As I lived quite locally, there was little need for me to board, which I was thankful for in my early years at Douglas, however you probably wouldn't believe me if I told you that when it came to my final years, I actually wanted to board along with the others!

Most importantly, there was music EVERYWHERE. On an initial tour, I remember hearing the music as I left the main school building and walked up the path that connected the main school to the music school. Back then, the music school was housed in a separate building from the main building and was adjoined by a little walkway at the back of the school. In later years as a pupil of Douglas, I never tired of hearing the music as I walked between the schools. In a sense, it was always comforting leaving the main school behind as you walked towards the music school, where you knew there would always be something interesting going on.

In my early visits, I remember noticing that the majority of the music school pupils kept to themselves. I supposed this was because they were connected on deeper level by their common love of music. I realise now that we were all outsiders to an extent, most of us having parted ways with our friends from previous schools. This however only strengthened the little cocoon of comfort and solidarity we built around ourselves and created unbreakable bonds that would go on to last for years after we left school.

When the first auditions came around, I had already visited the school a number of times and was beginning to feel more at ease being there. That day, as I walked along the corridor towards the audition room with Mrs Alves, I felt a tingle of nerves and excitement. I recognised that this was nothing like the anxiety I had been plagued with in my younger years, it was more a feeling of an erratic flurry of butterflies in my tummy.

I performed my audition pieces in front of a small, friendly panel of adjudicators with Mr Alves by my side accompanying me on piano. Ironic as it seems, having Mr Alves sitting there beside me in the minutes before the audition made me feel wholly at ease, despite knowing that my fate ultimately lay in his hands.

Following my audition, there would be a number of nerve-wracking weeks before I would find out whether or not I would be invited for a second audition. By this point, any initial qualms I'd had about attending music school had disappeared, and I now hoped more than anything that I'd be accepted. I had finally recognised that anxiety was like carrying an unnecessary weight around my neck, and that life didn't have to be like that anymore. I had also noticed that anytime I visited Douglas Academy, my worries seemed to disappear, and because no one there knew about my anxiety and what had gone before, I almost felt like I had an opportunity to reinvent myself entirely. I just had to get in first.

A few weeks later, I received the news I had been hoping for. My first audition had been a success, and I was invited to attend a second audition, which would take place the following month. Despite this being everything I had dreamt of, I still couldn't help but feel anxious at the prospect of staying away from my grandparents for a night. It was something I'd never done before, and I wasn't sure if I could do it. I remember laying in bed each night worrying. I worried about the audition and whether I'd get in. If I didn't get in, I worried what it would be like going to Clydebank High, where I knew I'd feel even more out of place than before. Most of all, I worried about staying overnight at the auditions and having an anxiety attack which usually involved my bursting into tears like a baby in front of everyone and embarrassing myself. I worried that if that happened, I'd have to be removed from the audition process which meant I wouldn't get in. In any case I thought they probably wouldn't want someone like me at the school if they knew what I was really like.

I must worried myself into a frenzy, because during one of our lessons together, Mrs Alves sat me down and explained that there was no need for me to be anxious about the auditions, and that if I didn't want to stay overnight, I really didn't have to. In the end, my grandparents collected me after the first day of auditions and took me back early the next morning for the second day. In later years, I'd look back and wonder why I'd been so worried over the auditions.

On the first day of the second auditions, everyone was allocated a chamber group to rehearse with. I was placed into a string quartet along with one other violinist, a violist and cellist, as is customary with string quartets. Although we were all initially nervous not knowing one another or what to expect, the quartet proved to be great fun, and was coached by a well-respected, amiable viola tutor who normally taught within Douglas.

On the last day of the auditions, there was a small chamber concert given by all candidates who had been a part of the process. It gave parents a chance to see what we had been up to over the past two days, and it gave all candidates the opportunity to perform in front of their families. For many of us, performing in front of an audience was quite new territory.

For the concert, our quartet performed Boccherini's String Quartet in E Major, Op. 11, No. 5, a popular classic that I was actually familiar with for once, having heard it featured in a popular television advert. During the performance, I remember looking over towards my gran sitting in the audience and remembering feeling panic rise in my throat as I saw tears in her eyes. What was wrong? Gran never cried. When I quizzed her on the way home, she told me that it was the performance that had brought her to tears, and that she wasn't crying because anything was wrong, but because she was so proud of me.

I would later find out that out of the four in our quartet, it would only be the viola player and myself who would be offered a place at the school.

Much of my life up until that point had been a rocky road, and the mental prison anxiety imposed over me had often robbed me of the joys I should have experienced in my childhood. Little did I know that afternoon as I sat miserably in my class of primary four, that Mrs Alves' visit would prove to be the first step in changing the course of my life. I hadn't realised how desperate I was to be given a fresh start, a new life, until I was actually sitting in the car on the way back from the second auditions. I realised then, that even if I didn't get into music school, I had still overcome a gargantuan personal hurdle. There was no turning back now. Either way, I resolved that I wasn't going to let anxiety rule my life anymore. This would be the start of the 'new me'.

The weeks that followed the second audition passed painstakingly slowly. At home we busied ourselves, although the tension in the air was palpable as my grandparents and I awaited the news we so hoped for. I had set my heart firmly on music school, and now I couldn't contemplate going anywhere else. There was no escaping the fact that if I didn't get in, it would be a huge blow to my confidence.

On just an ordinary day like any other, the phone rang around teatime. Gran went to answer it, and I could tell instantly by the tone of her voice it wasn't just anyone at the other end. My ears suddenly pricked up and papa hurried to mute the TV that had been blaring in the background. I sat and watched the colour rise in gran's cheeks as she listened carefully to whatever was being said on the other end. I had guessed by my gran's voice it was Mrs Alves, and I desperately tried to ignore my heart as it attempted to escape from my chest. Gran gasped, murmured her thanks and placed the phone back in its cradle. She paused for a moment before turning around and I held my breath. When she did, her eyes were sparkling wet and she whispered, "you're in".

Music School

Following my acceptance into music school and in the months leading up to the start of term, my grandparents began encouraging me to take more of an interest in classical music. Up until that point, I had virtually no knowledge of it, other than what I had learned in my violin lessons with Mrs Alves. From our initial visits to the school, it was clear that the pupils there had either come from musical families, or at the very least had some sort of grounding in classical music. When I say I knew nothing, I am not exaggerating.

In my family, despite the fact we all loved music, no one that I knew of was actually musical, unless you counted papa and his 'mouth organ'– the infamous harmonica which he would fondly refer to as his 'moothie' and would whip out given the slightest opportunity. I don't think this counts either, but I also grew up knowing the songs from Rogers & Hammerstein musicals like the back of my hand, and noticed from an early age that my taste in music was drastically different to the other kids at primary school. Whilst they would be learning dance routines to S Club 7 and Steps, I would be lip-syncing to Queen and had a huge poster of Michael Jackson on my wall. I also LOVED Disney music, but I'm guessing that isn't so unique because I mean, who doesn't...?

As an adult and a teacher myself, I recognise in my own sound that I tend to adopt a romantic, full-bodied sound akin to the likes of the Disney songs and musicals I grew up listening to. Call it heavy-handed, but I love nothing more than a good old healthy dollop of vibrato and cheesy portamento (an audible slide of the finger along the string when you change position).

Family-wise, I knew that on my mum's side I had an uncle who was a gifted guitarist, but I'd only met him a handful of times. I also vaguely remembered that my mum's dad, who had passed away before I was born, had been musical too. This being said, as far as I'm aware there were no classical musicians in the family, and certainly no classical music in our house before I started Douglas. I suppose gran and papa must have thought that if I stood the slightest chance of starting Douglas on par with the other pupils, I needed to be exposed to a lot more classical music. They wasted no time.

One day I came home from school and was surprised to find a large box of CDs sitting on my bedroom dresser. It was a full A-Z collection of composers and their most famous works. Beside the box stood a large hi-fi that had been assembled to accompany the music collection. The hi-fi was a sleek black and silver design, and when it was plugged in the lights shone bright blue. I loved it instantly. It held and rotated something like up to six disks at a time, and as I began to devour the music collection, I quickly became familiar with each composer and the stylistic differences between the Romantic, Classical and Baroque eras. It soon became clear to me which composers I favoured most, and whose music most resonated with me.

I just loved flicking through those disks, choosing whatever I felt suited my mood that day. I often pretended that I was on stage either playing my violin or attempting to lip-sync some of the operatic works. Sometimes I'd even get my violin out and try to play along, especially if I had ordered the music from the music shop beforehand. I have to admit I am slightly cringing at my younger self here, but looking back, immersing myself in this way was not only developing my understanding around music and history, but pretending to perform was paving the way for a time when I would be performing on stage for real. It turned out there would be plenty of that at Douglas.

Gran must have signed up to a mailing list, because 'What's On' brochures started arriving through the post from the Glasgow Royal Concert Hall. I have particularly fond memories of gran and I flicking through the brochure selecting the concerts that took our fancy. Anything involving a violinist was booked up without question. In and around that time, we went to watch performances from some of the most prominent solo violinists of our generation, including Nigel Kennedy, Maxim Vengerov and Daniel Bell.

It ended up being something we would do together for years to come. I will never forget how excited I felt getting all dressed up for our girls' night. Papa would drop us both off outside the large, concert hall beside Buchanan Galleries, and off we would trot in deep conversation about the evening's entertainment. Classical music concerts weren't really papa's thing, but nevertheless he was more than happy to drop us ladies off so we could enjoy an evening's entertainment with beautiful music in beautiful surroundings.

Some of the first concerts we went to see together were the RSNO Children's Classic Concerts. The audience would be packed full of children and their parents, and the buzz of excitement in the auditorium was palpable. These concerts would generally feature popular classics, and the conductor would make a point of selecting players of the orchestra to give a demonstration on their instruments, which in turn allowed the young audience to hear what that particular instrument sounded like. One concert which stands out in my memory was called, 'Why Should Children Have All The Fun?' It was a gala concert put together to raise money for the Children's Classic Concerts series and featured performances from Yehudi Menuhin's sister Yaltah Menuhin, who was a virtuoso pianist, and a thirteen-year-old Scottish violinist called Nicola Benedetti. There were also performances from the Orchestra of Scottish Opera, Bearsden Choir and the Newtongrange Silver Band.

As many of you will know, these days Nicola Benedetti is considered to be one of the finest violinists of our generation. Back then, aged thirteen, she was just three years older than I was. I remember watching in awe as she stood in a crimson red gown at the Glasgow Royal Concert Hall, and performed a piece of music considered to be one of the most challenging works ever written for the violin, the *Carmen Fantasy* by Pablo de Sarasate. Nicola left the whole audience in raptures and exited the stage to thunderous applause. How lucky I feel now to be able to say I went to see one of Nicola Benedetti's earliest concerts. Even back then, it was clear she was destined for great success.

Around the same time as the hi-fi and cd collection, I came home from school another day, and I could tell by my grandparents' faces that they had been up to something again. They smiled conspiratorially, and I looked quizzically from one to the other. Without a word, they led me into my bedroom. To my utter astonishment, there stood the shiniest, most beautiful thing I'd ever seen. I gasped. It was my very own upright piano. Sitting in front of it, was a luxurious-looking mahogany stool, cushioned in red velvet. I would later realise to my delight that the seat lifted so you could store your music inside. I ran to them, thanking each one profusely. Gran explained that as I would be expected to learn piano as a second study when I started Douglas, there was now no excuse for me not to practise. The piano quickly became a prized possession of mine, of course along with my violin. Not having faintest idea how to play, I was more than happy to just sit and tinkle and make up my own little tunes until the time came for me to receive proper lessons.

When the time did come for me to begin piano lessons at Douglas, I was more than eager. Piano lessons with my lovely teacher, Mrs Dylan became a highlight of the week. It was fun to learn something entirely new on an entirely different instrument. I soon realised that my favourite pieces to play on the piano were by the composers Chopin, Mozart and in particular, Debussy. Learning to play the piano gave me a whole other outlet and would prove to be a godsend on the days where I felt like I was getting nowhere fast with my violin practice. For me, piano was always pleasure, and practising never felt like work. I spent six years playing the piano at Douglas, although these days, I regret letting it fall by the wayside, as it inevitably did when the violin began to take up most of my time.

Anna Markov

In the initial months of my first year at Douglas, my violin teacher was Ernest Pegg, then-leader of the RSNO. Mr Pegg had also been a panel member at the second auditions, and afterwards had decided that he would come into the school to teach myself and one other violinist called Kirsten Michaels, who was an older girl I remembered standing out at the auditions.

Ernest Pegg was an esteemed leader and highly regarded teacher with a wealth of experience under his belt. The initial few lessons we had together were productive, however the main downside was that Ernest's job would take him away for long periods at a time. This often meant that Kirsten and I could be without a teacher for weeks or even months on end.

Anna Markov came into our lives and changed it forever. I met her on a day I was supposed to be having a lesson with Ernest, but for whatever reason he'd had to cancel. As I peered through the small glass window of the practice room to see if he had arrived yet, to my surprise it was Mr Alves who stood inside, talking to a young woman with a violin in her hand. As they laughed and chattered, I wondered if I had made a mistake with the rooms, but suddenly Mr Alves spun around and beckoned me inside. As I stepped into the small practice room, Mr Alves introduced the young violinist as Anna Markov, and explained that from now on, she would be periodically filling in for Ernest. Anna beamed over at me and I couldn't help but notice that she had the most exquisite brown eyes I'd ever seen. Anna couldn't have been much taller than myself at 4'11, and even from those brief initial moments, I sensed she was going to be different from any other teacher I'd come across. Once initial introductions were exchanged, Anna wasted no time in getting started with the lesson.

After that first lesson, Anna began to step in for Ernest more and more, until eventually Kirsten and I we were receiving weekly lessons from her. In a couple of short months, my violin playing and technique had improved rapidly. When Ernest retired a few months later, I was thrilled to learn that Anna had officially become both Kirsten's violin teacher and mine.

The thing about Anna is that, aside from her charm and wit (which I've seen work on even the stuffiest teachers who would visibly thaw in her presence), and those intense brown eyes (which have the ability to simultaneously terrify and disarm you if you haven't practised enough that week), is that she is a wildly talented violinist. To this day, I have yet to hear someone play the way Anna can. She can make a series of scales sound like a concert performance and can make even the most challenging techniques on the violin look as natural as breathing. Anna was never slow in letting you know if you were slacking. I remember hearing the words "sloppy practice", "unacceptable" and "you are three minutes late, Hazel" on more than one occasion, much to the amusement of my friends who would snigger if ever they heard Anna reprimanding me in public. Of course, it was never personal and Anna's displeasure never lasted long.

I would later learn that Anna had begun her studies in Scotland but moved to the United States at a young age to study with a famous professor who now teaches at the Julliard School in New York. Following this, Anna studied in Russia and then London under the legendary Felix Andrievsky.

Anna put a lot of time and effort into our lessons together, and always went out of her way to provide extra tuition when she could. She really believed in me, and often praised my abilities. One lesson a week became two, as she began teaching me from her home every Sunday, asking for nothing in return except hard work and commitment. Two lessons a week could become three or more, as everyone began to receive an extra lesson called "practice support", which took place every week at the halls of residence. Anna also began coaching the small ensembles I was in, including a string quartet, which I led.

Anna quickly established the reputation of being the best violin teacher in the school and was becoming increasingly sought-after. By the time I left school, she had around seven or eight violin pupils, bearing in mind that the music school was a small place.

Looking back, I don't think Douglas Academy was quite prepared for the petite powerhouse that was Anna Markov. She instantly shook the place into the

21st century and injected a sense of energy and vibrancy that no one realised was missing until she arrived. When I think back to my first encounter with Anna, I can't help but feel that on some level, everything really is meant to be. I often look back and wonder how on earth I managed to go from having such a rocky start in life, to suddenly finding myself in a music school, being taught by one of the finest violin teachers in the UK.

A Word About Technique

To say Anna puts strong focus on her students' violin technique is putting it lightly, and for this I will be eternally grateful. As a youngster, Anna recognised that time was of the essence and didn't waste a minute in developing my own technique through a series of left hand finger exercises and right arm bowing techniques.

The thing about technique on a musical instrument is that it forms the very basis of everything you are able to eventually do on that instrument. It's actually a bit like building a house in that if you have good, strong foundations from the very start, this generally results in having a structurally sound and secure building. Therefore, it goes without saying that if you focus on establishing good foundations from the outset, and are satisfied that these are secure, you can then start to work on and hone in on the finer details. In the instance of violin playing, the foundations are scales and studies and the finer details are the phrasing and musicality of a piece of music. Of course, this is a rather generalised statement and obviously it's really never too soon to begin working on phrasing and playing musically, but hopefully you see the point.

As with many skills in life, the earlier you begin, the better. This isn't to say that you can't improve and build upon your technique as an adult or teen, because you absolutely can, but ideally, the younger you begin, the better. Very often, technique on the violin is best established as a child, when the brain is most malleable, and joints and muscles are supple. It's a well-known fact that we learn new information most easily when we are children, and you may have heard the expression that children's brains are like sponges. Therefore with this in mind, the ideal scenario for a teacher would be to acquire the student and start them off at as early an age as they are able to stand still and take instruction. Even before this point, the sooner a child can be exposed to music (even if it's just listening), the better. Most of the violin greats began between the ages of three and six, and this is no coincidence.

Naturally, it depends on the child and each child is different, but if you begin learning at an early age, you will probably never remember a time when you didn't play. Because of this, playing an instrument becomes as easy as walking, and as natural as breathing.

I wasn't quite this fortunate, and began at the age of eight, which is the most common age for children learning an instrument at school. This being said, I was so thirsty for information and so keen to learn, that what I lacked in age, I made up for in practice. It was still young enough for me to be able to pick up on technique quickly firstly from Mrs Alves, and then from Anna Markov when I began studying with her at the age of eleven.

Life At Douglas

School life at Douglas Academy really was some of the happiest times of my life. It was there that I was able to grow into myself not only as a musician, but also as an individual. I had a wonderful group of friends who were all on the same journey of self-discovery with me, and it was impossible to ever feel lonely there.

As Douglas pupils, we were all given the opportunity to challenge and step out of our respective comfort zones, whilst having the support of the school and the staff behind us. Creativity and opinions were encouraged and valued by the school, and as there were only a small number of pupils, it meant the staff were able to place true emphasis on the individual, offering extra support wherever needed. We were treated like equals, our individual talents celebrated.

As a pupil at Douglas, aside from the academic side of things, our musical education also revolved around rehearsals and performances. Much to the envy of the rest of the school, each of us were assigned early lunch passes, which allowed us to take lunch earlier than our peers over in the main school. The reason for this was that every lunchtime usually involved some sort of rehearsal or performance.

To give you an idea, on Mondays we would have choir practice, Tuesdays I think, were free (but it didn't stop us making up an excuse to get into the lunch hall early), Wednesdays were orchestra, Thursdays were wind band and Fridays we would gather together for a lunchtime recital where the music school pupils would perform in front of teachers and peers.

In addition to our lunchtime activities, we would usually have after school rehearsals, which would go on until about 5pm. For me, Tuesday evenings were my favourite as we had Chamber Orchestra with Mr Alves, who was my all-time favourite teacher. On Wednesday evenings, it was ensemble practice, and on Thursdays it was First Orchestra.

At the beginning of the year, each of us would be allocated a chamber group and for me as a violinist, it would usually be a string quartet or trio. Second orchestra was for first and second years, if I remember correctly, and First Orchestra, was for the third years and above. I actually attended First Orchestra in my second year, which amused my friends and they would playfully tease me. It wasn't uncommon for the younger pupils to find themselves in the older groups if their abilities matched the older pupils. We also had Junior Choir and Senior Choir, similar to the First and Second Orchestra scenario. Before you ask, no I wasn't asked to join senior choir early – if you know me at all, you'll know I'm not a gifted singer at all; certainly no Charlotte Church! As I said, there was music EVERYWHERE, and I just couldn't get enough of it.

~◈~

Aside from lunchtime and after school activities, there would be music classes timetabled throughout the week and there were always concerts to prepare for. Concerts included chamber music evenings, open evenings, composition evenings and end of term concerts. The concert at Christmas was particularly spectacular as it would take place in St Paul's Church in Milngavie, and on the day of the concert, the pupils involved would get the day off school. Basically, we would all be ferried to and from the church in large coaches, depending on the rehearsals we were involved in. We felt like celebrities and felt extremely smug to be having a day off school so close to Christmas. I honestly wonder what the teachers in the main school must have thought of us. Taxis to school and coaches to rehearsals, it was all great fun! The Christmas concert rehearsals always felt a bit magical, and even now, I can remember feeling the festive buzz in the air.

Despite there being such a strong emphasis placed on performance at music school, the atmosphere there was never pressurised. I think because everyone did it, it was just accepted as part and parcel of being a pupil of the music school. Solo and group performances were always fun, and that's how they were supposed to be. That's not to say we didn't feel nervous sometimes, because I know I'm not alone in saying that we did, but somehow the relaxed setting managed keep us feeling safe and cocooned in our little bubble. There was never a situation where you would be reprimanded or demoralized if a performance didn't go well. It was all just taken in our stride, there was no bullying, and we championed and encouraged one another, as we recognised we were all in it together. If you ask me, this environment was single-handedly to the credit of Mr Alves, who devotedly cultivated this unique setting.

Mr Alves retired the year we left and in the years that followed, my friends and I would agree how extremely blessed we were to have had Mr Alves throughout our time at Douglas. Not only was Mr Alves a fine role model at such a pivotal and impressionable moment in our young lives; it was also clear he cared deeply about his role within the school and music school as a whole. Everyone knew he held a special place in his heart for his pupils.

There were also specialist music exams. Aside from attending graded exams on our second study (as on our primary instruments we had often surpassed graded exams early on), we were also all timetabled to give two solo recitals a term, one of which was a technical assessment.

Oh, the dreaded technical! At the beginning of the term, Mr Alves would distribute a printout with a blank grid upon it, and our teachers would fill it in and hand it back to Mr Alves, who would then use it in the technical. In the weeks before the technical, and during our lessons, our respective teachers would populate the grid with the various scales and arpeggios we had been working on, along with a series of articulations. After the technical assessment, we would then perform a piece of music, akin to the standard recital, although in contrast to the standard recital (which would just be a case of you and an accompanist performing a piece of music in front of the music school staff and pupils), the technical involved Mr Alves being seated at a table directly in front of you, firing at random the various scales, arpeggios and articulations from the grid your teacher had earlier provided him with.

Despite the relaxed environment, the technical often put the fear of God into even the most seasoned performers, although for me personally, whilst these exams were nerve-wracking for sure, they were never too awful as Anna had drummed into me my scales and studies from the get-go. Mr Alves and the technical assessment could never be as scary as Anna on a bad day, so I suppose in that sense she did me a favour!

Concerts

During my years at Douglas, I took part in many concerts, some of which took place out with the school itself. In my second year, Mr Alves asked me to perform a solo for the Glasgow Chamber of Commerce at the breath-taking Merchants House of Glasgow, in George Square. It was very formal event, and Mr Alves had only chosen a couple of us to represent the school that evening. I remember how grown-up I felt when I was told the dress code was non-school uniform, and gran surprising me with a black velvet, retro-style dress with a sweetheart neckline and a netted underskirt that she'd picked up from a vintage shop in Partick. Aside from having to take the shoulders in a little as my frame was so slender, it was perfect in every way. I still have that dress, and although it doesn't fit me anymore (sob!), I just couldn't bear to throw it away.

That evening, I performed one of gran's favourite pieces, "Scène de Ballet", by Charles Auguste de Bériot. It was a piece of music that I had discovered early on in my musical education, and had featured on one of the many CDs gran had bought for me. The CD in particular was Itzhak Perlman's "Concertos From My Childhood", which quickly became my favourite CD. On the front cover was a sepia-toned photograph of Perlman as a child, his eyes closed and fully absorbed in playing his violin. I remember listening to each track back-to-back, way before I ever met Anna, and feeling almost bereft that I would never be able to play the way he did, even as a child. I suppose this is why Anna coming into my life when she did felt like the stars had aligned for me, as quickly I realised she was the only person who could ever teach me how to play the way I wanted to.

My rendition of "Scène de Ballet" proved to be popular, and I ended up playing it on a few occasions after the Chamber of Commerce concert, including one of the Douglas Academy open evenings. As for the CD, I made it my mission to be able to play every piece on there by the time I left school, and although I didn't perform all of them in concert, I could happily say I achieved my goal.

Every year there was a "Douglas Academy Annual Recital", which was held at the Royal Scottish Academy of Music and Drama (now the Royal Conservatoire of Scotland), in Glasgow. All pupils were involved in the concert, although as it was one of the school's higher-profile events, it tended to be that the younger pupils performed in smaller ensembles, and solo performances were usually reserved for the older, more experienced performers. During my first two years at Douglas, as expected, older pupils gave the violin solo, however by my third year, much to my delight, it was me who was chosen.

I remember feeling extremely nervous as I stood on stage in the large, resonant concert hall and played to an audience packed full of peers, parents and teachers. Despite my nerves, I still managed to perform from memory "Chaconne in G Minor" by Tomaso Antonio Vitali. Whilst there is no doubting that the Chaconne is a stunningly beautiful piece of music which really showcases violin and performer's ability, it features some rather exposed and technically tricky moments for the player, which, if tackled incorrectly can really make or break the performance. This is why it not only makes for a very effective showpiece, but it can also be used as a great tool within violin lessons, as it features a range of both left and right hand techniques which can then be implemented within the music itself.

Around my fourth year I performed "Suite for Two Violins and Piano Op. 71" by Moritz Moszkowski for the very first "Centres of Excellence Concert", which was a high-profile event held at "The Hub" on Royal Mile in Edinburgh, and compered by Sally Magnusson. The following year and for the second of these concerts, I performed the violin solo "Sabre Dance" by Aram Khachaturian - a fast-paced challenging showpiece transcribed by the great American Violinist, Jascha Heifetz. This concert took place at the Glasgow City Halls, which I remember being jam-packed. The third of these concerts took place in my final year, and at that time myself along with three others were part of a string quartet, led by myself and coached by Anna. The others were strong players too, and the second violinist was also one of Anna's pupils. Because of this, we were able to really let go and enjoy the performance, confident in each other's ability having worked together and performed consistently for months beforehand. The concert was held at Strathpeffer in the Highlands and travelling there by coach and getting to stay overnight in a large hotel was particularly exciting for everyone, especially for my second violinist and I, who were close friends and got to share a room!

For the concert, we played "String Quartet No. 4 Op 18 in C Minor" by Ludwig van Beethoven. I remember there being less pressure for this concert and I was able to enjoy my surroundings more than I had in the previous two years, when I'd performed solo. Whilst I loved nothing more than performing solo, being a member of a quartet (or any ensemble for that matter) means that the whole experience of performing is shared, as opposed to when it's all on you. It was a lovely way to spend my last ever Centres of Excellence concert.

Charterhouse Festival

As with many musical establishments, masterclasses and recitals were a frequent occurrence at Douglas. The school was often visited by some of the most prominent figures in the music industry, and as pupils there, we met and engaged with these figures on a regular basis.

One masterclass that stands out in my memory and which proved to be pivotal in my education was given by the violin teacher, Natasha Boyarsky, who once upon a time had taught Nicola Benedetti at the prestigious Yehudi Menuhin School in Surrey. At this point, I was sixteen years old and in my fifth year at school.

For the masterclass, I performed the first movement from Samuel Barber's Violin Concerto for Natasha and the rest of the music school. It was a piece I'd learned years previous, and one I had performed comfortably many times. Despite this, I remember feeling intensely nervous to be performing for Natasha, who boasted a multitude of world-acclaimed alumni. After the recital, as is customary with all masterclasses, there was a public lesson delivered by Natasha based on the performance I had given.

~❖~

In the end I built the whole thing up in my head, so that when the time actually came to perform, I remember feeling markedly disconnected from my surroundings, and the whole experience felt like I was in some sort of fuzzy dream. Nevertheless, I managed to perform my piece from beginning to end without any blips and was able to engage on some level with Natasha during the lesson. The reality, however, was that I felt completely out of whack and was unable to focus on much else other than how nervous I felt.

Afterwards, I felt extremely disappointed, and scolded myself for letting nerves get in the way of what might have been a once-in-a-lifetime opportunity. I wasn't sure what had happened that day, as usually I embraced any opportunity to perform. As I agonised over the experience later that evening with gran, she told me not to think any more about it, and just to chalk the whole thing down to experience. Whilst we were having this conversation, the phone rang. It was Anna. She had called to tell me that Natasha had been impressed with my performance earlier that day and had invited me to attend one-to-one violin lessons with her that summer, at the British Isles Music Festival held at Charterhouse School in Surrey.

The festival was a residential course focused around chamber music, solo performance and masterclasses, and was designed to celebrate emerging young musicians. The age brackets were eighteen to thirty-two, however there were a number of younger students, including myself at age sixteen.

The course proved to be extremely beneficial for me in various ways. Aside from receiving daily tuition from

Natasha and other respected music tutors within the industry, the course also gave me the chance to mix with a completely different pool of musicians, many of whom had come from the Menuhin and Purcell schools (which are two of the most prestigious music schools in the world). As there was such a broad age spectrum, the course gave me the opportunity to study and play alongside some much older students, many of whom were already well into their degrees at music colleges all around the UK, and some students had even come from overseas. In the ten days I spent there, my playing transcended to a whole new level, and with every day that passed, my confidence grew.

Admittedly, aside from the world-class tuition I was receiving, Charterhouse also turned out to be some of the best fun I have ever had. Being one of the youngest students there, but still old enough to 'socialise', I remember experiencing my first taste of rebelliousness and revelled in the idea of hanging out with a much more 'sophisticated and older' crowd. Thankfully by that point, I happily boarded with the others, whilst my grandparents rented a B&B close-by, and because I was having so much fun, I think for the whole time I was there I only saw my grandparents once! Throughout the course, I continued to receive daily one-to-one lessons with Natasha whilst expanding my knowledge around chamber music and working within ensembles.

Music College

My final year at Douglas Academy was my best yet. By this point, I had been able to drop the subjects I wasn't interested in and focus on the things I loved which were languages and music. This meant I took lessons in Spanish, Italian, French, and of course, Music. As a side note, I used to always say that if I hadn't gone to music college, I would have definitely gone to university to study languages, as for some reason they came quite naturally to me.

I would have back-to-back music practice sessions timetabled in by Mr Alves, and this gave me a chance to really focus on the next chapter that would soon be approaching - music college auditions.

Unlike some of my music school friends who had decided to do something other than music at university, there was no question in my mind that after Douglas, I would continue on to music college, and in particular my dream was to study at the Guildhall School of Music and Drama in London. I remember being in my first or second year at Douglas, and Mr Alves announcing that one of our best flautists, Francesca had been offered a full scholarship there to study. Upon hearing this (before the days of Google), I persuaded my grandparents to order prospectuses for this college, and after learning that the establishment bragged a throng of famous alumni, I decided that if I worked hard enough I would go there once I left Douglas.

By the time I reached my sixth and final year at school, the desire to audition for Guildhall was definitely still there, however I was also interested in potentially studying at the Royal College of Music in London with Natasha, the professor I'd received daily lessons from at Charterhouse the year before. In addition to this, many of my friends were auditioning for the Royal Northern in Manchester. Manchester was definitely attractive to me at that time, as it wasn't quite as far away as London, and had a number of excellent teachers, who had reputations of turning out many fine musicians. By the time it came to submitting applications, I was excited by all three of these options, so I decided I would just audition for all of them and see what happened.

Unfortunately, things didn't go much further than that for me. In the end, I was persuaded to audition for the music college I least wanted to study at, which was the Royal Scottish Academy of Music and Drama (now the Royal Conservatoire of Scotland). Before we go any further, I will refer to this college as the 'RSAMD' for short, as this was what it was called back then.

The RSAMD was furthest down on my list for many reasons. For one, whilst it had the reputation of being excellent for a variety of other instruments - including brass, woodwind and vocal and opera studies - for strings, at least back then in my opinion, there was much more excitement happening elsewhere in the UK. Into the bargain, I was desperate to gain some independence and to move away from home, especially after my experiences at Charterhouse. My grandparents and I had spoken about it and they encouraged me to chase my dreams and celebrated this desire for independence, explaining that we would work it all out logistically and financially when the time came.

Ultimately though, Anna stressed to both my grandparents and myself that I was much too young to be going down to London on my own, and at seventeen, she expressed concern that I wouldn't be able to cope either emotionally or financially. Naturally we all trusted Anna's judgement, so we eventually decided that it was probably best to just listen to her. She went on to explain that I would be given all the extra time and 'extra opportunities' I desired because I was Scottish; her theory being that Scottish people promoted Scottish talent, and just look at what it had done for Nicky (Nicola Benedetti).

Despite strongly disagreeing that I wouldn't be able to cope away from home, I supposed some of what Anna said did make sense, and in any case I was used to doing as I was told. Reluctantly, I put my dreams and my intuition to one side and decided to listen to everyone around me.

I remember all of my friends' surprise when I told them I wouldn't be auditioning for London after all, given my initial excitement at the prospect. I even had one close friend in particular, a viola player I had met at the Douglas auditions (if you'll remember, from that very early quartet), whom I had played with and performed alongside since that very day, telling me I HAD to get away from Scotland and had to follow my gut and go to London. Despite this, I obediently listened to everyone else around me and obediently narrowed down my choices completely to The Royal Northern in Manchester (for experience) and for the RSAMD in Glasgow, where I would be Anna's first and only pupil.

In the months before auditions began, Anna explained that she would be able to give me much more one-to-one lesson time than I'd receive from any of the colleges down south. This was what ultimately convinced me to stay in Scotland as I knew Anna would stay true to her word as she had always gone above and beyond for me. Anna went on to explain that aside from the idea that Scottish people promoted Scottish talent, there would be more opportunities in general, quite simply because there was a smaller pool of musicians in Scotland.

Whilst all this made sense, I still couldn't help but feel disappointed that I wasn't going to be able to spread my wings like I'd hoped, and to live down in the big smoke where it was vibrant, gritty and where I could forget about my past and reinvent myself. I admit, it was a heavily romanticised notion, but it doesn't take away from the fact my heart was elsewhere when I auditioned for the RSAMD.

Even when I went to the Northern and felt the buzz there, it felt electric, new and exciting. Manchester was so metropolitan, so busy and loud and grimy – I loved it. The RSAMD in Glasgow didn't feel like much of an adventure as I'd been inside the building loads of times. Even with my friends, I had been into Glasgow on numerous occasions, and the prospect of living with my grandparents for a further four years when I could be living my dream in London just didn't excite me much.

I suppose that you could say I was a typical teenager in the sense that I felt rather entitled and wholly misunderstood.

Nevertheless, Anna really was an outstanding and passionate teacher, who had dedicated so much of her time to educating and nurturing me. She had given me extra time and commitment when she didn't have to, and I recognised that everything I had achieved as a violinist up until that point was down to her alone. I decided that it probably wouldn't be so bad remaining in Scotland for a while longer. I knew I still had so much to learn, and perhaps Anna was right; perhaps it was in my best interest to stay put for the time being. I resolved to make the very best of things and throw myself into the idea of studying at the RSAMD. I would continue to work hard alongside Anna and put my dreams of living in London to one side for a bit. I could always do a Masters there after graduation.

Much to my delight, I was accepted to study at the Royal Northern in Manchester, but quickly put it to the back of my mind as I knew I wouldn't be going there. At least the upside to studying at the RSAMD was that, following my audition with the Head of Strings and Deputy Head of Strings, I had been asked to wait behind and attend a further mini-audition before the Head and Deputy Head of the RSAMD who together made up a scholarship panel.

A week or so after auditioning for the scholarship panel, I was told that in addition to my acceptance to study at the RSAMD, I would also be receiving a full scholarship to study there. For me, this was a huge achievement and somewhat of a relief financially for my family, for had I not received the scholarship, I would have had to apply for a student loan, as there was no other way I could finance my studies.

Just as I started to put my focus and energies towards life as a student of the RSAMD, and my grandparents had proudly told everyone we knew I'd been awarded a scholarship; a few months down the line we were told that I wouldn't be receiving a scholarship after all. I can't remember all the ins and outs of it, but it was a pretty sharp shock without much of an explanation. I know that not everyone had their scholarships revoked, so perhaps they had over-stretched themselves and had promised more scholarships than they could give out. Nevertheless, it was a massive kick in the teeth and a huge blow to my confidence.

As I said before, I can't remember the details of why this happened (perhaps it's because the explanation we were given at the time was rather vague), but I do know that not too long after my audition, a senior member of staff at the RSAMD left his post unexpectedly, and I remember rumours circulating around concerns over the RSAMD's finances. On a personal note, whilst having my scholarship revoked certainly left a bitter taste in my mouth, I tied not to dwell on the disappointment and humiliation of it all. I didn't want to let a minor blip like this cast a shadow over how excited I had been up until this point, so I picked myself up, dusted myself down and applied for the student loan!

It didn't take long to make friends. The music circle is quite a small one, and because I was already a member of NYOS (National Youth Orchestra of Scotland), I had already encountered many familiar names and faces during my first few days there. In any case, I wasn't worried. I guessed that this was what Freshers' Week was all about, and couldn't wait to get stuck into the events that had been planned.

By the time Freshers' Week was over, I had found a fun group of people and we all quickly became friends. After that, I spent most of first year finding my feet within this new and exciting environment. I'm not going to lie; initially it was all a bit of a jolly. I was getting used to this whole new concept of being independent and the sense of freedom that came with it was intoxicating.

After a few months, we had all finally begun to settle into our respective routines and it was probably at this point where I started to sense my first feelings of unease within the college. It had quickly become clear amongst the violinists, that if you didn't have a certain senior member of staff as your teacher, you would go virtually unnoticed. It became common knowledge that this member of staff's pupils received additional perks at the RSAMD, including securing the best seats in the college orchestra, and were also allowed numerous opportunities to work outwith the academy on external projects which took place all over Scotland and even abroad. Very often, on the String Department notice board, photos would appear of external projects that this member of staff had been involved in along with his pupils - the rest of us were oblivious that the event had occurred in the first place. These students were introduced to some of the most celebrated and influential figures in the music industry at that time, and it quickly became clear to everyone that unless you were this person's pupil, you would really struggle to be noticed.

Some pupils even transferred from other teachers and attempted to work their way up the ranks.

It really hit me hard, coming from somewhere like Douglas where everyone's efforts were recognised and talents encouraged, to finding myself somewhere where no matter what I did, even though I was at the top of my game and a consistent high-achiever with high marks, I felt like I would never be good enough unless I had a certain teacher.

And so, I felt I had to work extra hard to be recognised. I realise isn't necessarily a bad thing, but in retrospect I'm not sure that it was an entirely healthy mind-set. Despite my lessons with Anna continuing to move from strength to strength, I very quickly becoming disillusioned as a student at the RSAMD. I began jamming in practice whenever I could, early in the morning before college and staying behind at college after hours to catch up on more practice. It was an erratic, unfocused kind of practice, and looking back, I was really beginning to lose my sense of self. I obsessively worked on technique, cramming hours and hours of practice into single sittings, without breaks. Because of this, my technique was getting better and better, and in my second year; I was awarded the highest mark of the year in my technical exams. Despite all of this, for some reason I couldn't seem to be able to feel or interpret music anymore, which was what I had always been so good at. I became increasingly confused and for the life of me couldn't understand why I was able to play difficult passages of music without any problems technically, but was no longer able to use my imagination to tell stories through my music, something that once upon a time had made me so happy.

It honestly felt like something had died within me, and in our lessons, Anna often became frustrated and said things like "you should be good at this, this music has you written all over it!" Although I couldn't feel music anymore, I continued to receive high marks in performances, which I suppose was all that mattered, right? Wrong. The high marks never seemed to matter anyway, because I still wasn't getting noticed by that one member of staff who mattered, whose students were rewarded with leading and co-leading the various orchestras at college.

Greece, Anyone...?

I had become miserable and jaded, and by my third year I was looking into ways to transfer my degree to one of the colleges in London. It wasn't looking possible and I knew it would seriously disrupt my degree, along with my finances and my mental health.

Instead, Anna encouraged me to take part in performance opportunities out with the RSAMD and urged me to get in touch with an old friend of hers, Professor Hu Kun, a well-known violin teacher who taught at the Royal Academy of Music in London. Anna suggested that I take lessons with him, in the hope that it would provide me with a wider perspective, and hopefully unlock my musicality again, whilst regaining some of my confidence.

After reaching out to Kun via email, I swiftly received a reply. I was in luck, and he suggested I join him in Greece for the Rhodes International Music Festival that summer. Much like Charterhouse back in my Douglas days, I had a few months to prepare repertoire and studies to take along with me to Rhodes, where I would receive daily lessons from Kun, over a period of ten days.

~❖~

Rhodes International Music Festival

So, here I was, travelling to Greece that summer, and to be honest the fact I would be going there knowing no one didn't particularly faze me. With all the other stuff I'd done up until that point, from my audition for Douglas, to Charterhouse and the RSAMD, I was almost used to being a stranger among a group of people who already knew each other.

I found myself stepping off the plane at Athens International Airport in the early hours of a July morning. The sky had turned a dusky pink colour and the sweet smell of honeysuckle clung to the sticky, humid air.

Just one more connection and I would be touching down in Rhodes. Already Glasgow and the RSAMD were beginning to feel like a distant memory, as my mind began to drift off to more exciting things, like what would be happening over the next ten days. I revelled in the prospect of spending day after day in the sun, meeting and engaging with new and interesting people whilst getting to enjoy a different way of life for a while.

From what I'd seen on the festival's website, the hotel by all accounts was a five star luxury affair that overlooked the rugged, unspoilt Ixia Beach and the aquamarine waters of the Aegean Sea. It felt just like what I needed.

Upon my exit from the plane, I had initially followed my fellow passengers, but quickly realised that most were headed in the direction of baggage reclaim, meaning Athens was their final destination.

As the crowds dissipated, I suddenly found myself on my own, bar a few lone stragglers peppered around the Arrivals Lounge. As I began to search for signposts in this near-empty airport, it suddenly dawned on me that, although unsurprising, most of the signage was in Greek! For the first time since I'd left Glasgow, I felt the beginnings of anxiety settle in my bones as I realised that I was all alone in a foreign country, in the wee hours of the morning. As I continued to let mind continued wander down the garden path, a sequence of catastrophic thoughts sprung to mind that went something like this...

'The signage is in Greek! The Greek Language uses a whole different alphabet to the English one, meaning I can't even use my schoolgirl French, OR Italian, OR Spanish to get by! I can't call my grandparents... I'm going to miss my flight! WHAT AM I GOING TO DO???"

As the panic continued to rise like bile in my throat, I noticed the lone passengers had gone and there seemed to be no one around to ask. This was nothing like America I thought, where it had always been bustling and there were a myriad of signposts, all of which were in English.

I took a deep breath and told myself to get a grip; I needed to focus on the task at hand. As I stood in the silent Arrivals Lounge puzzling over which direction to take next, my ears suddenly pricked up as I heard faint chatter and laughter coming from somewhere around the corner to my right. I almost collapsed with relief, but quickly realised I'd have to get my skates on if I wanted to catch up with them. I followed the voices, my pace ever-quickening in an effort not to lose them. As I turned around the next bend with my heart thumping in my ears, I exhaled a silent prayer of thanks when I eventually spotted a group of young people strolling ahead, two of whom were holding violin cases.

There were four of them. Three boys and a girl, and they didn't look much older than I was. I continued to follow behind them at a distance, concluding that since two of them were carrying violins, it would be terribly unlucky on my part if they happened to be heading somewhere else other than the festival. I decided the risk was worth taking.

They unloaded their instruments onto the neighbouring empty chairs at our departure gate, and although I could hear them bantering and laughing amicably, they weren't quite close enough for me to identify their language. One of the boys looked up as I approached with my violin case and greeted me with a friendly smile, and at the same moment, the others turned round to examine me. Aside from us, the gate was virtually empty except for a few passengers who appeared to be locals.

As I prized my case from my shoulders and placed it down on the empty chair next to me, the boys introduced themselves. Two of them were Greek and one Albanian, but they spoke perfect English with attractive accents. The girl, who hadn't said a word up until this point, studied me suspiciously and remained in her seat, completely aloof. It made me feel nervous, but I pretended not to notice and smiled across at her and politely asked her name. She looked directly at me, clearly unconcerned with exchanging pleasantries. Without a smile, she stated in an unmistakably Russian accent that her name was Katy.

As the boys continued to talk amongst themselves, I tried to avoid eye contact with Katy who appeared to be sizing me up. Just as I was beginning to think we probably wouldn't be friends, she suddenly got up from where she was sitting and came over and sat down next to me. She said nothing initially, but we each exchanged a stiff smile, which was a start.

After our initial awkwardness, Katy and I quickly became inseparable. Although we came from completely different worlds, we found out that we actually had rather a lot in common, including the fact that we were both secretly nervous about what would be happening over the next ten days. As a fellow violinist, Katy and I bonded over all things violin-related, including the fact that we both actually liked to listen to music that wasn't exclusively classical. Into the bargain, Katy had the same wacky sense of humour I did, and because we shared a room together, we could often be found entertaining ourselves in our free time by doing dippy things like filming ourselves performing silly dances to silly songs and then falling about in stitches as we watched them together.

Katy was three years older than I was and studied violin performance with Alexandros Halapsis at the University of Indianapolis along with the boys I had first met at the airport. One of the boys on the course was also a violinist, and the other two were pianists. Alexandros Halapsis was the Art Director of the festival, and Katy had come on course to study with him and his father, Vladislav Halapsis who was also a well-known and respected violin teacher.

As promised, the hotel was magnificent. It was a vast, multi-storey structure with expansive grounds overlooking tastefully landscaped gardens at one end, and Ixia Beach on the other. Mornings consisted of large buffet breakfasts in the grand dining hall, followed by morning lessons.

Halapsis Teaches A Young Student

For the first few days whilst I waited for Kun to arrive, Vladislav Halapsis kindly included me in his own class, which meant that in addition to receiving daily lessons with him, I also had the privilege of observing him tutor other students, some of whom were very young. I remember how wonderfully kind and encouraging he was as he gently coached the younger pupils.

One little girl in particular couldn't have been more than six. She had arrived at the festival from Russia with her mum and her older brother. As I watched Halapsis teach this little girl every morning, I was struck early on by his tenderness and absolute consideration for the child's learning experience.

Halapsis kept the atmosphere positive and engaging at all times, never placing any pressure upon the young girl to get things right first time. He really seemed to understand what it took to gct thc most from his young student, totally unselfconscious as he broke his lessons down into little games and stories for the girl who would respond with cackles with joy, much to the delight of everyone observing.

Feeling inspired by how Halapsis set about creating the perfect learning environment for his youngest pupils, I decided to take what I'd learnt from watching him teach and implement the same approach in my own lessons. Create the right environment, and they will flourish.

Katy was taking lessons from Halapsis too, which was just as well, as he spoke practically no English, and I couldn't speak Russian or Greek. Katy took pleasure in being our translator (as Halapsis decided to conduct the lessons in Russian), and was happy to perch herself to one side in our lessons, interpreting when it was needed. Surprisingly though, it turned out that there was often little need for Katy's translations, as our common understanding of the music we were interpreting often did away with the need for spoken language; music being a form of language and conversation in its own right.

Lessons With Kun

After having our mornings filled with individual and group lessons, everyone was given a couple of hours free for lunch. After lunch there was an afternoon recital given by students in the main hall, and at night-time when it was cooler, there was an evening concert.

The evening concerts were usually given by our professors, famous musicians and international competition winners, many of whom had either come from, or had studied in Russia. The calibre of talent coming from Russia was astounding to me. Suddenly the world didn't seem so small anymore, and I realised there was much more to life than the RSAMD and its cliques, all of which seemed rather trivial after what I'd experienced in Rhodes that summer.

When Hu Kun eventually arrived in Rhodes, I took to him instantly. Like many of the other teachers there, he had brought his own family with him on holiday. This to me felt reassuring, to know that despite being a famous violin teacher, he was just human like the rest of us, enjoying a working holiday with the family. If he had kids, he surely couldn't be that scary...?

Although Kun was firm, there was no pressure. Aside from myself, he was only teaching two other students at the festival, a pair of siblings much younger than myself, who had come over from London with their mother.

Kun gave me much to consider during our lessons together, and praised my technical ability and interpretation of the music I had prepared. Above all else, in gaining a different teacher's perspective on my playing, I was able to expand my mind and my ideas around music, which enabled me to reach a greater level of maturity in my playing. The ten days I spent in Rhodes really proved to be the confidence boost I needed.

I returned from Rhodes revitalised and ready to take on whatever the RSAMD had in store for me. I was going into my third year, and the experiences I'd had over the summer meant I was going in with a completely fresh perspective. I had made friends for life in Rhodes that summer, and although I missed everyone - Katy in particular - Alexandros Halapsis had suggested I study in Greece for a Masters. Although I wasn't sure about Greece for my Masters, I suddenly felt like I had options. Only two years to go and I would be graduating with a Bachelor's degree in Music.

Scottish Ensemble

Unfortunately, the upbeat feeling didn't last very long. No sooner was I back at the RSAMD than I started to feel suffocated again. I was past the stage of wanting to go out to parties and socialise, and was only too happy at the end of the day when I could board the train at Glasgow Queen Street and doze off in a cosy train all the way back home, where I could escape from it all.

It was around this time that I met Andy, who would later become my husband. We quickly became inseparable and spent most of our free time together.

As for college, despite feeling jaded, I was still a strong, reliable player with a good reputation. Because of this, I continued to receive more opportunities at college than I would have otherwise. I was selected to do opera on more than one occasion, along with string ensemble (both of which were reserved for the stronger players) and a number of other activities; but somehow, I still felt unfulfilled. I couldn't quite put my finger on it, it just felt as though something was missing.

Things were about to change though. A few months after I returned from my trip to Rhodes, I found myself in one of the Glasgow Royal Concert Hall's suites auditioning for the Director of Scottish Ensemble, Jonathan Morton. I had decided to audition for a place in Scottish Ensemble's side-by-side project, where a small number of outstanding young musicians from the RSAMD were, following a successful audition, invited to join Scottish Ensemble in a series of concerts to be held all over Scotland. The tour lasted around a week, and there were to be concerts held in Aberdeen, Dundee, Edinburgh, Inverness and Perth.

Up until this point, although I'd auditioned for many things over the years, I had never auditioned for a professional ensemble. Scottish Ensemble had been my favourite ensemble since I was a child, and I remember on more than one occasion sitting in the audience with my gran, watching starry eyed as Jonathan Morton and his wife, Clio Gould lit up the stage in concerts alongside the vibrant players of Scottish Ensemble. To be awarded a place on this project would be a dream come true, and it felt like there was a lot riding on this audition for me.

I have to admit, when I met Jonathan Morton, I was pretty star struck. I'd only ever watched him perform on stage, so to be actually talking with him face to face, never mind auditioning for his ensemble, was rather a big deal. I needn't have worried though, as Jonathan instantly put me at ease with his down to earth approach and friendly demeanour. What's more, to my surprise and delight he seemed to love my audition, and actually applauded the orchestral excerpts I had prepared. I left the audition grinning from ear to ear, and in that moment, I felt like I was walking on air. Could this be it? I wondered. Could this be the moment I had been waiting for?

I was working at Junior Academy the Saturday when Scottish Ensemble's list of successful applicants went up on the String Department notice board. I took a deep breath as I scrolled down the list. As I put my finger to paper my heart stopped as it landed on my name. There it was in black and white, along with a small group of others from the auditions. A wave of gratitude flooded over me. I had to double check once more before calling Anna to tell her the news. I remember taking my lunch break that day and decided I would take myself somewhere special to celebrate. I went to my favourite café, 'Café Wander' on West George Street and ordered myself a full English breakfast with a pot of tea and a cake. Things were on the up.

The tour itself was a challenging yet rewarding experience, and it really provided me an insight into what it would be like work within a professional ensemble. It was an honour to play alongside such accomplished musicians. The members of Scottish Ensemble wholeheartedly welcomed our small group from the RSAMD, and ensured that we were made to feel very much a part of their circle.

I couldn't believe my luck touring with an ensemble I'd admired since my childhood. Rehearsing and performing alongside professional musicians helped to solidify in my mind that I really did want to become a professional musician after college, and reminded me that despite how dire I felt at times, there was most certainly life and success waiting for me after graduation.

Injury Strikes

At some point during my tour with Scottish Ensemble, I started experiencing pain in my left hand when I played. I didn't think much of it and continued to play, ignoring and pushing through the discomfort. I was sure I had experienced something like this years before, and with a bit of rest it had just gone away by itself. The thing was, because I was on tour I couldn't rest, so I pushed it to the back of my mind and made a mental note to address it after the tour.

In the weeks following my acceptance into the Scottish Ensemble project, I was finally getting noticed. I continued to score highly in performance and technical exams, and finally I was being selected for extra projects within college, which was something I'd always wanted. Although there was a degree of pressure that came along with this newfound popularity, it felt good to be sought-after, and I said yes to virtually everything in an effort to please everyone.

As I stood backstage, warming up to go on stage with Scottish Ensemble, the pain in my hand was almost unbearable. Determined not to let pain hold me back,

I popped a couple of ibuprofen, and managed to push through the concert, resolving I would have a good rest after the tour.

By the end of the tour, I could hardly play on my left hand. By this point, I was undeniably worried. I suspected tendonitis, a common yet incapacitating injury, but quickly dismissed this idea. Admittedly, in my arrogance, I told myself that it was only people with poor technique who contracted tendonitis, so surely it couldn't happen to me.

Around this moment, I guiltily thought back to my practice cramming sessions. I seemed to have trained myself into working at my best under pressure, often achieving great results when working towards fast approaching deadlines. Most of the time, I neglected properly warming up before practice sessions, and cooling down by stretching after a session. I thought I was fine, because up until that point I had gotten away with it.

After taking a week away from playing to rest, I remember going into my first lesson after the tour and Anna putting the Prokofiev Violin Concerto No. 2 in G Minor up on the music stand in front of me. She explained how she would be performing this piece in a concert soon, and she thought it was just the piece for me to get my teeth into. As we began to read through the piece together, I started to feel the pain again in my left hand again but tried to ignore it. A couple of lines into the piece, the pain was unbearable, and forced me to stop. As I tried to continue, I simply couldn't. The pain was so severe that I couldn't bear to put any pressure on it whatsoever. This was when I realised I was in real trouble, because I could no longer could play on my left hand at all.

Anna was deeply concerned and suggested I take two weeks off to recuperate. It felt strange being told by Anna of all people not to practise, but I had no choice but to take her advice. After two weeks of no playing whatsoever, I went back to my lesson and attempted to play again. Things were still no better, if anything they were worse. Anna suggested another couple of weeks off. Two weeks turned into three, three into four, and by then it was clear that this injury wasn't going away itself; I needed physio.

I was well into the second term of my third year by this point, the penultimate year to my degree, where every mark counted towards the degree itself. Luckily, I managed to get in touch with BAPAM (British Association for Performing Arts Medicine) and was awarded funding to spend on one of their specialist performing arts physiotherapists. For the next year I attended physiotherapy with Dr Sara Watkins and had to cancel everything I had agreed to do at college. The strain of having to let people down was almost unbearable, especially as I had worked so hard to build a reputation and gain people's trust.

I often wondered if I would ever recover from this physically, mentally and professionally. I felt defective and ashamed that I had let this happen to me.

I was off playing for at least nine months, and barely had reason to even go into college. I felt demoralised and utterly useless. Most of all, I felt as though I had let everyone down and that everything I had worked towards had been for nothing. I had pushed myself to the limit and now to my dismay, I could barely play a simple nursery rhyme in first position without recoiling in pain. I frequently needed to take anti-inflammatory painkillers, as the area on the inside of my index finger would become visibly red and hot to touch. It was stiff, and I struggled especially in the mornings and evenings. Even turning handles on doors were an issue. I just felt utterly dire.

Realising how depressed I had become, Gran booked us both a last minute holiday to Tuscany, and although I took my violin with me, I didn't play it once. I remember wondering if I'd ever be able to play again, and mourned the idea that just as I was beginning to become noticed, this was happening.

Clawing It Back

I still don't know how I managed it. I think it was the humiliation I would have felt at being held back a year, but somehow I still managed to do a final recital in the last term of my third year. Had I been unable to do this, I would have almost certainly been held back, which was unthinkable to me. I had returned from Italy in the May, still unable to play anything, and in the July, I still somehow managed to do the recital, which was around thirty minutes long. I had resolved to sit that exam no matter what, and told myself I just had to get through it to pass the year.

After Italy, Anna and I had resumed lessons slowly; picking a programme that was easy for me to learn quickly and was as light as possible on my left hand. That year, I performed the Debussy's Violin Sonata in G Minor, Handel's Violin Sonata in D Major (HWV 371) and a 21st Century piece of music for solo violin called 'In Flight' by the British composer, Stephen Davismoon. I remember standing in the large concert hall at the academy, feeling entirely vulnerable. I remember my legs were like jelly, as my knees knocked together in an effort to hold me upright. I hadn't played properly in months, yet here I was sitting the most important exam of the year.

~◈~

Despite my injury, my nerves and lack of practice, I still managed to achieve a high grade for my final recital, higher than some of my peers. Granted, it wasn't as high as it had been in previous years, but it had definitely gone better than I was expecting. I remember feeling triumphant knowing that despite my setbacks, I had somehow managed to pass third year and I would be returning the following term on par with the rest of my peers.

Fourth Year

I would like to be able to say that following my third year recital, my tendonitis disappeared and I was fully healed, but it wasn't quite as simple as that. In terms of physical recovery, whilst I had made a vast improvement, it would be another year until I was completely pain free. Into the bargain, I had to 're-learn' the violin almost from scratch, which meant endless practice sessions spent in front of the mirror correcting my posture and re-moulding my left hand in such a way so as to avoid further injuries in the future. How I felt emotionally was a whole other story, and recovery in this department would prove a lot more challenging.

Life in the early days after tendonitis wasn't what I expected. I imagined that as soon as I was able to play again, life would resume as normal and I'd be able to pick up where I had left off, which in my case was just after the tour with Scottish Ensemble. Logically, the next steps for me would be auditioning for other programmes similar to Scottish Ensemble, and then eventually auditioning for extra work within professional orchestras with the aim of securing something more permanent long-term.

A few months into my fourth and final year, it became clear that 'picking up where I'd left off' wasn't going to be quite as simple as I'd imagined. This was less to do with my physical capabilities and more to do with how I felt emotionally after having to learn the violin again from scratch. What I hadn't bargained for was how utterly demoralised I'd feel and although it's hard to admit, I couldn't help but wonder why it had to happen to me. It all just felt very unfair and was extremely hard for me to accept and come to terms with.

Somewhere along the way, I had developed the unhelpful habit of being able to shut down my emotions entirely when it came to music. It happened whenever I took my violin out of its case, and although I recognised how my negative thoughts affected my mood and my ability to play musically, I had no idea how to overcome it. It just felt like a grey cloud would settle over me every time I tried to play and no matter how hard I tried to make it budge, it just wouldn't.

I had gone from someone who adored music with every fragment of my being, to feeling completely indifferent and numb around it.

Lessons with Anna had become increasingly strained, and although I was still able to play technically very well with minimal discomfort, something was still missing. I felt like a shadow of my former self, a completely hollow being. I couldn't feel music anymore, and whilst I knew it was scary, I just couldn't muster the energy to feel concerned. It couldn't have been easy for Anna as my teacher, as she had witnessed my love for music and confidence grow at Douglas, and then completely spiral downwards at music college. Anna tried to help break down my barriers, but they were much too high, and eventually we were both left feeling frustrated, confused and defeated. Anna, by this point, had established herself the most sought-after violin teacher at the RSAMD and now had plenty of capable students.

I was just as glad, as it took the focus and the pressure off me.

Looking back, I was much too hard on myself. Instead of applauding everything I'd overcome in such a short space of time, I scolded myself for not bouncing back quickly enough. I should have treated myself with the love and compassion I deserved, but instead I mentally beat myself up, telling myself I was useless and unworthy. Instead of celebrating my efforts in overcoming what could have been career-ending injury whilst giving myself time and permission to heal physically and emotionally, I wrote myself off and told myself my dreams were over.

Around this time, Andy and I broke up. My Andy, who had stood by me all through my injury and the toughest of times had decided he wanted to apply for an officers' course in the Royal Marines which would take him away to the south of England for the foreseeable future. I understood that he had to go and figure out his path, much in the same way as I did, but nevertheless I was heartbroken and our breakup just added to the confusion I was already feeling.

At some point it dawned on me that I was at a total loss as to what I was going to do with my life. I didn't have any opportunities waiting for me after music college. I didn't have job to go to and didn't feel as though I had any other skills outwith music. I had invested all my time, money and efforts into becoming a professional musician, never for one second imagining I would ever want to do anything else. Having once been so sure I would do a Masters in London after my Undergraduate degree in Glasgow, all I knew now was that I didn't want to look at the violin again for as long as I lived. In a moment of panic, I decided to apply for law school once I graduated from the RSAMD.

Final Recital

By the time my final fourth year recital came around, I just wanted it to be over and done with, with minimal excitement or fuss. We had been encouraged to invite family and friends to these recitals, and someone somewhere along the line had even mentioned that if we didn't at least make an effort to find audience members, we'd be marked down. To this day I'm not sure where this idea originated, because it later transpired that many of my friends had enjoyed rather low-key recitals, but when I heard that we could be marked down for something so trivial, I panicked. Losing marks was the last thing I wanted (or needed), so about a week before the recital, I logged in to Facebook and frantically invited all my friends on there, including old friends from Douglas I hadn't seen in years. I sincerely hoped that no one would turn up, and I could at least be seen to be making an effort.

Unfortunately, my plan backfired on a mighty scale. As I made my way backstage to warm up in the minutes before my recital, I stopped dead in my tracks. There, in the auditorium foyer stood dozens of familiar faces that had come out to support me. I should have felt overjoyed and supported, but instead I felt sick to my stomach. What had I done?

~❖~

Unlike my third year recital where I had prepared relatively easy pieces, Anna and I had chosen a technically demanding and energetic programme for my final recital. The recital was forty minutes long, and each piece of music was lengthy and strenuous for both the violin and the piano, meaning there was little opportunity to relax into the performance. Normally, this kind of scenario wouldn't have fazed me, but as it had only been a year since the injury, I felt I had to call upon all the energy and concentration I could muster just to get through the performance. The piano accompaniments were challenging and at times tricky to marry up with the violin, which only added to my nerves on the night of the recital. It was all so vastly different to how I had been playing just a year previously, but somehow, I still failed to accept just how far I had come. That year, my recital programme consisted of Karen Khachaturian's Sonata Op.1 for violin and piano, the Leclair Violin Sonata in D Major, Op.9 No.1 and the Ravel "Tzigane".

My recital was the last one of the day at around 8pm. It was hot and sticky inside the small auditorium, and I remember nodding my acknowledgment to the many familiar faces as I walked out onto the stage. I felt I owed it to them all to put on the biggest and best performance they had ever seen from me, and that it was my duty to prove how quickly I'd bounced back following such a debilitating injury. I'm sure many of them were expecting the young and vibrant young violinist from Douglas who had been awarded the scholarship, but thee person they had come to see instead was someone entirely different, someone I barely knew myself. I felt like I would snap under the weight of pressure, but I knew I had no one to blame other than myself. I cursed myself for being so stupid in thinking no one would turn up. I couldn't help but ache for Andy right there in that moment, wishing I could look up and miraculously see the kind, non-judgemental face I knew so well. I felt a pang in my chest as I lifted my violin to play and tried to focus on the music.

The recital was okay. Nothing special or spectacular, and I suppose in spite of how I was feeling, it ran rather smoothly, without any major mishaps. Needless to say, I wasn't happy with the performance. During the recital, it had been a constant battle to fend off an overwhelming sense of exhaustion that had settled over me from the moment I had walked on stage. Whilst I tried to focus on the music, a string of negative thoughts invaded my headspace, menacingly posing the questions I often pushed to the back of my mind, like, what did I really have to show after six years at a specialist music school and then a further four at music college? Was this really it? What happens next? Will I ever get over this? Who even am I? Whilst I tried my very best to focus on the performance at hand, these persistent internal voices re-played the same questions over and over again.

A few weeks later, our results came in and I was given a mediocre mark in line with most of the other violinists in the year. Anna would later tell me that I hadn't performed well on stage. Hearing this from the person I admired most was cutting but it wasn't a surprise. I wasn't sure what I was going to do with my life, but in those moments, I was certain I wouldn't be picking up the violin again for a very long time.

I tried to remind myself to celebrate everything I had overcome, and to forget about all the unpleasant stuff that was now out of my control. The main thing was that I had done it, and I was finally free. I had managed to graduate on time with a 2:1 degree from the Royal Scottish Academy of Music and Drama. Yes, I had been on track for a first class all the way up until my injury struck, but none of this mattered anymore. I was just glad that I was now more or less pain-free and had made it through to the end without quitting, which would have been the easy way out.

Beyond College

That summer turned out a lot better than I expected. Admittedly, there were a few weeks of moping around as I tried to figure out my life, but eventually I began to enjoy the novelty of being able to do whatever I wanted without having to worry about ever setting foot inside the RSAMD again. What's more, things were actually on the up. Andy and I got back together, and I had been accepted to study law at three different universities. The small issue of having limited finances and there being no available funding for my course didn't matter. By that time I'd realised I wasn't ready to throw myself into full-time study again, and somewhere deep down I knew I wasn't quite ready to give up on music just yet. Nevertheless, applying and being accepted into university to do something other than music gave me a great sense of achievement and was something different to focus on when I needed it most.

Throughout life's ups and downs, I continued to teach the violin. I think this is what probably kept me sane during those difficult years. It was uplifting to catch up with my pupils each week and to see them progress steadily. As I watched them grow in ability and confidence, it was reassuring to know that at least I was doing something right in helping them achieve their goals and ambitions.

Most of my pupils back then had come through word of mouth, but sometimes I advertised cheaply on Gumtree and in the local newspaper. I taught complete beginners along with existing players of all ages and abilities. By the time I graduated, I had established a good pupil base from my grandparents' home and had plans to continue in the same way when I moved in with Andy.

Yes, you read it right; Andy and I decided to move in together! Shortly after graduation, we decided to get back together. Andy (naturally) realised he couldn't live without me, and I admitted I had been miserable without him.

At that time, I was still living with my grandparents near Glasgow, whilst Andy, because of work, was based in Fife. It made more sense for me to move, and aside from my violin pupils (who I would continue teach from my grandparents' home), I didn't have anything tying me to Glasgow. Fife wasn't so far away and it was easy enough to drive through to Glasgow whenever I needed to.

Anna and I remained relatively close in the months after graduation. Unfortunately, we went on to lose touch over the years, but I will be eternally grateful for all she has done for me. Now that I am older, I realise how difficult it must have been for Anna to witness me spiral after injury. As far as I know, Anna continues to teach and perform internationally. She remains one of the most sought-after violin teachers in the UK.

Unexpected Event

Marriage was always on the cards for us. Andy and I often spoke about it; when it might happen, what our wedding would be like and where we would eventually live. Andy always wanted two kids, and I wanted at least ten. Andy would always protest, and each time I would describe my vision of big Christmases, with our grown-up children and grandchildren sitting around a big table, tucking into Christmas dinner, chattering and laughing jovially. There would be a log fire crackling away in the corner and multiple stockings hanging on the mantelpiece. As I gazed into space dreamily, Andy would scoff. He was the sensible one and said we would never be able to afford ten kids, so I would just have settle on the idea of two, maybe three as an absolute maximum.

For Andy, being in the military always came with the possibility of having to move around the country. Drafts can be tricky and are sometimes unpredictable because it usually just depends who is needed and where. Many drafts last for a number of years, whilst some can be as short as six months, so whilst there was always a chance Andy could be drafted, we tried not to dwell on it.

~❖~

In May 2013, Andy went ahead and bought his very first flat in Dunfermline. I moved in with him on a part-time basis, dividing my time between the flat and my grandparents' home in Glasgow, where I continued to teach my violin pupils. In the three years we had been together, Andy and I had never lived together, so I decided to ease myself in gradually, hence the part-time arrangement. Although I had sworn never to set foot inside the RSAMD once I had graduated, that didn't last long, and I found myself there working regularly with my string quartet and violin/harp duo. In the months before I graduated, the RSAMD had become a much nicer place to be. The tense atmosphere had lifted and on the whole the students seemed a lot happier. After graduation, my angst towards the place had subsided considerably and I was finally able to accept that my own feelings had dictated many of my experiences there. It was a bitter pill to swallow, but I had to make peace with the fact that it wasn't fair to blame the RSAMD as a whole for what I'd experienced, and that I had to take ownership for some of it too. With graduation behind me, my sole focus now was learning how to fall in love with music and my violin again.

In terms of practicality, everyone agreed that it was sensible for Andy to get a foot on the property ladder. Even when he inevitably did get drafted, his plan was to rent out the flat until he returned to Scotland, which was always his intention. Back then, there did seem to be an unfortunate pattern amongst some of Andy's colleagues, that as soon as someone bought a house nearby, they would receive a draft at short notice. I'm sure it wasn't intentional, and more of just an unfortunate coincidence. In any case, we weren't worried. A draft for Andy wasn't on the agenda, and the odds of us falling victim to such a scenario seemed unlikely.

No prizes for guessing what happened next. We had hardly been in the flat two weeks and, by the look on Andy's face when he returned home from work one day, I could tell straight away that something was wrong. It was a beautiful sunny day, so he suggested talking a walk in the nearby park. Although I had an inkling of what was coming, I said nothing, hoping I was wrong. We sat on a park bench in silence; the two of us taking in our surroundings, smiling as we watched some kids happily run around nearby. The unspoken words of what was about to come hung in the air. Eventually Andy came out with it. That day at work, he had been told he had received a draft and would be starting a new life and a new job in Portsmouth in early September. It was already late May. My head was buzzing. We had barely three months before our life, as we knew it, would change.

We couldn't afford to rent a property down south, and we knew we couldn't be apart again. The only other option was to get married and move into military married quarters. Whilst we knew we wanted this one day, neither of us felt particularly ready to undertake such a serious commitment; after all, we were only twenty-two and twenty-four respectively. It quickly became apparent that we had no other choice if we wanted to stay together, as we couldn't bear the idea of being in a long-distance relationship. There really was only one option left, and once it was agreed, the months that followed were a whirlwind.

A week after our visit to the park, we announced our engagement. By the 3rd August, we were married, much to the delight of my Catholic grandparents. By late September, we found ourselves moving into a small married quarter in Gosport, almost four hundred and sixty miles away from my grandparents' home in Glasgow, and in the weeks that followed, I found myself wondering just what I had gotten myself into.

A Crash Course In Adulthood

The months that followed were rocky. At twenty-two, I was terribly homesick and missed my friends and my grandparents. I also missed my work and the pupils I had left behind. I missed my quartet and my duo. Most of all, I missed who I was just months prior. Suddenly, I'd gone from being someone who was fresh out of college to being someone's wife, in a place where I couldn't have told you where the nearest shop was. It had all happened so fast. Don't get me wrong, I loved my new husband and I wholeheartedly wanted to be his wife, I just wasn't sure where to begin in this strange new place that I knew so little of. Refusing to bask in self-pity, I began to run daily. Although I wasn't yet familiar with the area, I knew there was a pebble beach nearby, so I dug out my iPod and resolved to get fit.

It was a hot summer and the fresh sea air did everything for my complexion. I was becoming tanned, lean and I felt healthier than I'd ever been. When gran next came to visit, she would comment on how well I looked. Next, I decided I had taken enough time off work; so, I set aside time to tackle my CV, something I had been putting off. I chipped away at it, editing until it was as good as I could make it. I wasted no time in writing to the local music service in Hampshire to see if there were any vacancies for a violin teacher. I scrolled and scrolled through various job vacancies, many of which were miles away from where I lived. It didn't matter; I would drive.

I lost count of how many jobs I had applied for. Weeks passed, and I tried not to feel discouraged when rejections came rolling in, or worse still, I would hear nothing at all. I realised that part of the trouble was that I that I was completely unknown with an unproven track record in this area. My glowing references from the RSAMD didn't seem to count for much here and in any case; there was no escaping the fact that it was a dire time for musicians in general, many of whom had jobs which had been affected by funding cuts to the arts. The stark reality was that teaching positions were becoming fewer and further between. There just weren't enough jobs to go around.

After months of no success, I took matters into my own hands. After all, I was an extremely able violinist and a good teacher; there was really no good reason why I shouldn't be teaching. I started to place adverts on Gumtree and the local newspaper, and Andy started spreading the word around at work. I decided that if government cuts to the arts were going to be an issue for me securing work, I would write to independent schools instead.

I fired up my laptop and Google searched independent schools within a twenty-mile radius of where we lived. I wrote to all of them and waited. After a few weeks I had still heard nothing, and this is when the real panic set in. I had finally reached the conclusion that I had literally no music contacts here, no friends and no family. I knew no one here except Andy. I was hundreds of miles away from home, living a completely new and different life to the one I had had just weeks previously. I couldn't find a job. What on earth was I going to do? I was stuck here for the foreseeable future and I had given up everything to be here.

It got to the point where most days I found myself in tears. Andy tried to help, but there was little he could do to console me. I knew how guilty he felt for bringing me down here, and that just made me feel even more wretched because none of it was his fault.

Dr Jane Oakland

One day, an idea came to me from nowhere. Instantly, I was drawn again to my laptop, suddenly remembering that BAPAM (British Association for Performing Arts Medicine) had helped me in the past when I was injured during college. It dawned on me that maybe it wasn't just physical issues BAPAM helped with, maybe they helped with mental health issues too. After a quick search on their website, my thoughts were confirmed; BAPAM helped professionals overcome mental health issues related to creative practice. I took a deep breath and composed an email to them, explaining everything that had happened throughout college, along with my move to Hampshire and the struggle to find work.

It didn't take long for BAPAM to come back to me with a reply. They assured me that they could indeed help, and that I was actually eligible to receive funding. Their closest practitioner lived in Dorset, around an hour away. It didn't matter to me. I was already deeply grateful for BAPAM's response, and only too happy to travel for any help that was available.

Before I go any further, I honestly cannot begin to thank this wonderful charity enough for the amount of help it has given me throughout the years. Had it not been for the funding that BAPAM provided the first-time round, which allowed me to be treated for tendonitis by one of their specialist osteopaths, I very much doubt I would be playing today. Two years later and here I was again, being given what felt like another chance, thanks to BAPAM.

The practitioner BAPAM put me in touch with was Doctor Jane Oakland, a music psychologist and performance coach. Without a shadow of a doubt, our work together saved me in those first two years down south. I visited her every six weeks or so and during these sessions I was finally able to explore the feelings and emotions I had continuously suppressed during my years at music college. It felt like I was finally able to piece together where I had gone wrong and why I felt such a sense of animosity towards music and my violin. In a safe, comforting space, we talked about my hopes, dreams, disappointments and fears not only relating to music, but also relating to life up until that point. Jane helped me acknowledge that I hadn't really felt at one with my violin since my Douglas days and that it was clear I had lost so much of my confidence and sense of self. Becoming injured had been the final straw.

For the first few sessions, Jane didn't make me play the violin; instead it sat in its case, and we just talked. It was during these times that I found myself opening up to Jane about things that I hadn't ever told anyone. It was as though my mind had been subconsciously shelving and sifting for quite some time and, all of a sudden, here I was purging everything that had built up over the years. Often, I would find myself in tears, but Jane reassured me that it was good to cry and that I needed to let it all out to be able to move forward.

In turn, things began to pick up at home. I was happier, which meant Andy was happier. As the weeks progressed, Jane gently persuaded me to take my violin out from its case. Initially I just sat with the violin on my lap, and Jane guided me through an exercise that involved actively allowing myself (for the first time in years) to actually 'feel' and work through any emotions that cropped up during this time. Whilst it was hard for me in the early days to open up, gradually it got easier, and ultimately proved to be a profoundly healing experience.

Eventually, there came a time when I felt ready to play for Jane and from her, I began to learn all about performance anxiety and how to overcome it. From our very first session, Jane had set me an end goal of performing in front of a live audience. Back then, I couldn't imagine ever being able to manage this again, but after a year of working together, I finally found myself ready to give it a go.

In addition to being a registered mental health practitioner, Dr Jane was also a professional singer, and continued to teach and perform regularly. At that time, she conducted the Bournemouth Male Voice Choir, and it just so happened that they were looking for someone to fill a solo spot for their summer concert.

It felt good to have a reason to practise again and preparing for the concert gave me something positive to focus on. I had decided on a programme of Mozart's Violin Concerto No. 4 in D Major (K. 218), 'Romanza Andaluza' Op. 22 No. 1 by Pablo de Sarasate and the 'Schindler's List' theme by John Williams.

Playing in the Bournemouth Male Voice Choir concert was the first time Andy had ever seen me perform, and what made it even more special was that gran had made it down to watch too. A few days before the concert, gran took me shopping and bought me a tasteful navy blue lace dress, explaining how important it was that I look and feel 'the part'. On the night of the concert from backstage, I watched two of the people I loved the most sit together in the second row of the large church. Suddenly, I felt a surge of love for them both, and a deep gratitude for them being there to support me.

The performance proved to be a roaring success, and I exited the stage to thunderous applause. I felt like I would simply burst with joy, as for the first time in years I had managed to focus on just my performance alone, without the negative internal chatter that had previously taken up permanent residence in my headspace. It felt exhilarating to be performing the way I did back in my Douglas days, and once again being able to tell stories through my music; something that before Jane, I feared I had lost forever. In those moments, I knew I'd cracked what for years had felt like an impossible, unknown code. The black cloud had finally lifted. I was back, and better than I ever had been.

After the concert, Jane and I kept in touch until I moved back to Scotland two years later. One of the last things I remember her saying to me was to never give up on the violin because I had a true ability to move an audience with my music. It goes without saying that 'Hazel's Violin School' wouldn't exist without Dr Jane

Oakland and the help and funding I received from BAPAM. If it hadn't been for their help during those difficult early years, I can say with certainty that I wouldn't be playing and teaching the violin today. BAPAM threw me a lifeline when I needed it most, and Jane helped me overcome an identity crisis whilst showing me how to love music and my violin again.

Primrose Hall School

At some point, during the course of my sessions with Jane, my mobile phone rang one day. Not recognising the number, I answered cautiously. A male's voice on the other end introduced himself as Geoffrey Darwin, Director of Music at Primrose Hall School, an independent school I had written to months prior. He explained that he was the Director of Music there, and had been impressed with my CV. He went on to explain that although there weren't any immediate positions for a violin teacher, he was still keen to meet and interview me for a potential opening.

I tried to conceal the surprise in my voice and supress the urge to do a happy dance right there and then. Could this really be happening? Someone liked my CV? I had an interview? At a private school?! Okay granted, he said there weren't any spots for a violin teacher yet, but it was at least a step in the right direction! I calmly accepted the invitation, and as soon as I hung up the phone I squealed with joy.

~❖~

After my interview with Mr Darwin, things started to happen very quickly. The interview had gone so well that even though there were no immediate positions, he felt that I could be just the person to trial a series of group beginner violin lessons for some of the school's youngest pupils.

I began to teach at Primrose Hall initially a couple of days a week, providing beginner violin lessons to small groups of five and six-year-olds. Although at that point I had no experience of group teaching, Mr Darwin showed unwavering confidence in me and allowed me full control over the lessons. Over time and with experience, I was able to learn which methods worked best for my young students and took great pleasure in seeing them improve each week.

At the end of each term there was a school concert, and parents came in their droves to fill a large gazebo that had been set up for the event in the school's expansive grounds. The concerts gave my young pupils a chance to show their parents and teachers what they had been learning in their violin lessons, and it always gave me such pride and joy to perform alongside them on stage. From the groups gradually came children who had enjoyed the group lessons so much that they wished to continue with me on a one-to-one basis. I also began to acquire some of the older, more advanced pupils, whose parents would pay for them to receive hour-long lessons with me. From there momentum gradually built, and before long I was teaching groups and individuals ranging from beginners to more advanced levels.

Uncertain Times

Just over a year into working at Primrose Hall, I discovered I was pregnant. Whilst the pregnancy was planned, it happened more quickly than either Andy or I had anticipated.

Our son, Jude was born on the 18th September 2015. I had had a tricky pregnancy, but we were just happy to have delivered a beautiful, healthy baby boy. There was a brief period of calm as we settled into our new roles as parents and I adjusted to maternity leave (with my intention being to return to Primrose Hall after Jude's first birthday). Life had other plans for us though, and six months later we were packing our lives up again as Andy had received a draft back up to Scotland. Whilst moving can be stressful at the best of times (let alone with a small child in tow), we were only too happy to be returning to the place we loved, where we could be nearer family and friends.

For a while we were between Glasgow and Fife, as Andy worked in Fife, but my grandparents lived on the outskirts of Glasgow. We had decided to buy our own place (eventually settling in Fife), as opposed to renting another married quarter, and my grandparents kindly let us live with them whilst we sorted everything out.

A few weeks after moving to Scotland, (whilst we were still staying with my grandparents), Andy was selected for a promotion at work. Whilst this was a great thing for him personally, professionally, and for the family financially, the timing couldn't have been worse. It meant that he had to return to Portsmouth for a course that was set to take him away for a further six months. It goes without saying that this was a really challenging and stressful time, but we were still determined to make the best of it and ride out the next few months.

Finally, we had found our 'perfect' home near Dunfermline in Fife. As Andy's promotion course was still in full swing in Portsmouth, I proceeded to move into the house alone with Jude, who had just turned one year old. Our new house was about a forty-five minute car journey away from my grandparents, and although they were both healthy and helped me in every way they could both physically and emotionally, they were both well into their eighties. I often found myself alone, trying to juggle everything at home whilst Andy lived and worked over four hundred miles away.

Eventually, Andy returned from his course. I thought we could finally begin the new chapter we had dreamt of, but sadly the stress of everything had taken its toll on Andy, and he felt he could no longer continue with our marriage.

Barely six months into our buying a new home, we found ourselves separating, and I felt like my heart had been ripped out of my chest. A few months later, Andy accepted another draft to Portsmouth that would take him away for the foreseeable future.

Looking back, I didn't think life could get any worse. I really felt like my whole world was crumbling around me. I was determined to stay strong for Jude who remained my sole focus, and gave me strength on the days where I felt like I wanted the ground to swallow me up. Throughout the time Andy spent in Portsmouth, he continued to travel to Scotland every other weekend to visit Jude, and although we weren't together, we were determined to remain civil for our son's sake.

Life was dark and hopeless in the first few months after Andy left. I often found it hard to lift my head from the pillow each morning, as I forced myself out of bed and put on a smile for Jude. He would always be standing in his cot, bright eyed and beaming, oblivious to what was going on around him. He was my very own little ray of sunshine. Nothing else mattered but him; this I was certain of. I was dizzy with the curveballs life had thrown at me, and the latest one had involved me unexpectedly finding myself as a single mum, in a brand new house in an area I was, yet again, unfamiliar with. I knew none of my neighbours, I had no friends, and my aging grandparents were a forty-five minute drive away. I honestly didn't know if I was coming or going.

In the months after Andy left, Jude and I often found ourselves living at my grandparents' home. Back then, I hated being on my own, and didn't want to be at home where it was big and quiet, and full of unpleasant reminders. My grandparents always made Jude and I feel welcome and safe. Their home was familiar, warm and comforting. In those months, I didn't know what to do with myself and couldn't envisage what the future held, but nothing could prepare me for what would happen next.

Tragedy

Eventually, there came a time when I had to force myself to go home. I knew I couldn't live with my grandparents forever, it wasn't practical and it wasn't fair on them. Gradually things became easier, and very slowly I learned to enjoy my own company. I'd even started to practise again in the evenings once Jude was in bed. Music and the violin continued to work its magic, and never failed to bring me moments of clarity and joy in the midst of any pain and suffering I felt. Since moving to Scotland, I only played for my own enjoyment and because of the change in direction my life had taken, I couldn't even begin to think about advertising for violin pupils. My priorities had certainly changed since becoming a single mum, and all of a sudden it felt vital that I look for a more stable job that would bring me a reliable source of income for when Jude and I inevitably had to move out of our home.

It was during this time that both my grandparents became very ill. It's much too raw for me to go into in any detail at this stage, but to summarise; they both suffered short (and very unexpected) illnesses and passed away within months of each other. Aside from Jude, they were really the only support I had, and in addition to being utterly heartbroken, I felt once again like the rug had been swept from under me. When Andy left, I couldn't imagine life becoming any worse, but here I was in the middle of my very own personal nightmare. I had felt alone when he left, but nothing could prepare me for the loneliness I felt now. I have never been so scared in my entire life.

Once again, I put all my energies and focus into raising and nurturing Jude. He was my reason for everything, for living, for breathing. He was my comfort, my best friend. The love I felt for this little boy knew no bounds, and I knew that I had to dig deep and to make everything okay for him, because he needed me and that was that. I decided that as long as he was okay, I would be okay. I wasted no time wallowing, and quickly made it my priority to find a secure job to create some sort of stability for us. I knew that I would have to shelf the violin for the time being, but somewhere deep down I knew this was all temporary, and that eventually when the time was right, I would open my very own violin school.

Life Goes On

Very fortunately, I was offered a job in Edinburgh as a legal PA. It was stable, interesting and I loved my boss. Around that time, I also found the most amazing child minder who agreed to take Jude for forty hours a week whilst I worked. Andy continued to see Jude on alternate weekends, travelling to Scotland by train and taking Jude to see his parents in the Lake District. Things were hard and heart wrenching at times, but very slowly things began to fall into a rhythm, and through work I was meeting new and interesting people and making new friends. As unbelievable as it sounds, through the routine of work and having a different focus, I was beginning to discover myself again and discovered a real sense of independence. I bleached my hair, began dating again (just for coffees because I was nowhere near ready for anything else) and even managed to discover a sense of peace and freedom at times.

For two years, this was my life. I was a single mum, working a full-time job and undertaking a long and arduous commute to and from work. Despite all this, I still managed to find joy in my days. My boss and I developed a close bond and to this day, I consider him to be a guiding light in my life. He stepped in as a mentor, a father figure and the voice of reason, all whilst allowing me to essentially learn on the job and entrusting me with every aspect of the business. For a brief spell, I loved my job so much that I started undertaking a specialist paralegal qualification in conveyancing. I was loving having a new challenge and the opportunity to use my brain in a completely different way. I was gaining impressive marks, and had almost completed the qualification, but I couldn't help but feel something was still missing.

I was beginning to realise that my life had finally begun to settle. I had weathered the storm and the sun was finally beginning to emerge through the clouds. I realised that I felt more at peace, and a hundred times happier with my life. I no longer felt like I needed a relationship to complete me, and instead was just happy to focus on myself, and co-parenting with Andy. Although I was still very much grieving for my grandparents, something within me had changed. I no longer felt lost or scared.

Things Get Broken To Get Better

Whilst working my nine to five job was something I loved and appreciated with my whole heart, I couldn't help but feel that I had suppressed an important part of myself. I desperately missed music and the violin, and I longed to teach again. It made me so sad that I no longer had any time to practise or play or teach. I felt caught up in the vicious cycle of work, often feeling exhausted by Friday and using the weekend to recover for Monday.

It was December 2019. The long hours, and the commute to and from work had begun to take its toll and I realised I'd been running on empty for quite some time. I was stressed out and needed a break. I was tired of feeling guilty for leaving Jude with a child minder all day every day, and felt like I was really missing out on being a mum. The past two years had begun to catch up with me and I could no longer hold down my grief for my grandparents.

After essentially suffering a mini breakdown, the doctor signed me off work with acute stress. I was off for two months and during this time I felt pretty confused. I wasn't sure what to do, whether to go back to work and have the same problems and worries or whether to resign. If I resigned, what would I do instead? Would I be able to teach, to build a pupil base all over again from scratch? Did I even have the energy?

After much deliberation and weeks of torment, I decided enough was enough and to quit my job. I longed to feel well again, to feel like me. It wasn't the first time I had felt lost and anxious about the future, but this time I decided to follow my heart and to do what I had always done in times of great stress and uncertainty. What was this thing? The violin. I picked it up and never looked back.

Epilogue

So, this brings me to today. Here I am, writing this book as the UK emerges from the lockdown of 2020. I'm feeling energised and positive. My business is quickly building, and music and the violin are a huge part of my life again. Most importantly, I get to spend quality time with Jude every single day. Things are calm, (well aside from running my own business!) but I realise this is what I am destined to do with my life; this is what I was born to do, and most of all, it's what I'm good at.

To be able to share my passion with the world is something I'm endlessly grateful for. By now, you have read my story and you know that I came from very humble beginnings. If it hadn't been for the opportunity of being given the violin to learn at school, I have no doubt my life would have turned out very differently. Because of the violin, I have made friends for life and have been presented opportunities I couldn't have imagined possible. Through music, I met the man who would eventually become my husband, and we had our beautiful son, Jude.

Being introduced to the violin at a young age gave me an outlet during many of the most challenging times in my life, and not only provided a welcome distraction at that time, but ultimately changed my destiny. Throughout my life, the violin has remained my constant, even during the times I wasn't able to play. It stuck by my side as a loyal companion and continues to do so to this day. Because of the fantastic tuition I received as a youngster, I have been able to re-visit the violin with ease, and still have the ability to play and teach at an advanced and professional level.

Because of the violin, I have been able to carve out my dream job, which involves sharing my passion of music and the violin with people from all over the world. Through my business, I create opportunities for people of all ages and abilities, from varying backgrounds. I am especially passionate about bringing the violin to those who might not normally be in a position to learn, and as mentioned before this could be for a number of reasons. I want to show that no matter what your circumstances are, irrespective of where you live, your age, ethnicity, background or finances that there IS a way you can learn the violin well and affordably. I also want to reiterate just how much the violin has transformed my mental health, and how I believe it can do the same for you, whether you are an adult going through tough times or you are the parent of a child who is struggling. I want you to know that the violin can be used as an outlet and a source of support that can be accessed throughout the course of your life.

All you have to do is take a leap of faith and never look back.

To access the FREE Beginner's INTRODUCTORY COURSE click here

https://hazelsviolinschool.com/beginners-introductory-course/

A Little Note Of Positivity

After two years, Andy moved back up to Scotland and continues to live and work here to this day. Throughout everything, Andy remained a dedicated and devoted father to Jude, and after moving here was always happy to come over and help out whenever he could. He eventually sought therapy for what he now calls a 'breakdown'. I am happy and grateful to be able to say that we have decided to work towards reconciliation and have high hopes for the future.

Acknowledgements

Thank you to everyone who made this possible. To Paul Wakefield for his instruction and support. To Andy, for agreeing to take Jude off my hands when I needed the time to write. Thank you to my wonderful friend Ellie, for providing emotional support in the form of endless coffees, and for agreeing to read through all the bumf without judgement. Thank you to my tutors throughout the years, especially Anna Markov and Mr and Mrs Alves – these aren't your real names but you know who you are. Thank you to BAPAM and Dr Jane Oakland, without whom I would have given up long ago. Thank you to the staff at Primrose Hall and for the Director of Music there for taking a chance on me. Thank you to my solicitor boss who threw me a lifeline – you know who you are. Thanks to Taira for always being there for me. Thanks to Simon and Liz for being a true source of support from across the pond. Thank you to my pupils past and present, and to those who continue to support Hazel's Violin School. I love and appreciate you all.

About Me

Originally from Glasgow, I now life in Fife, Scotland. My son, Jude is now 5-years-old and aside from my business, he takes up most of my time (and energy)! Aside from teaching the violin and working on my business, I love playing the violin for fun and often find that hours can pass without my realising it. I also love spending time with friends, travelling and anything to do with food as I'm the biggest foodie ever. My dream is to one day travel the world as I love exploring different countries, cultures and FOODS!

Resource Links

Hazel's Violin School (for lessons, courses and membership)

www.hazelsviolinschool.com

Music, Anxiety & Me – How To Transform Your Life By Learning The Violin!

www.musicanxietyandme.com

Social Media Links:

Facebook: https://www.facebook.com/hazelsviolinschool/?modal=admin_todo_tour

Instagram: https://www.instagram.com/hazelsviolinschool/

LinkedIn: https://www.linkedin.com/in/hazel-spain-3bb3a01b3/

YouTube: https://www.youtube.com/watch?v=LKUrnHcMTE4

Twitter https://twitter.com/hazelsviolinsch

ACCESS THE FREE BONUS BEGINNER'S VIOLIN COURSE HERE!

https://hazelsviolinschool.com/beginners-introductory-course/

Printed in Great Britain
by Amazon